I0095049

"This timely publication by Nancy Brown opens up an opportunity for introspection and realization that early childhood offers a window of opportunity to instill the fundamentals that each individual needs to become agents of the culture of peace and non-violence. Her book articulates convincingly that helping children gain a global citizen's perspective in the early childhood years is essential for a safer, saner and sustainable world. Recommendations and suggestions she offers are practical, relevant and valuable to teachers and managers of early childhood schools in different countries and regions of the world."

Ambassador Anwarul K. Chowdhury, *Founder of the Global Movement for The Culture of Peace (GMCoP); Member, Executive Committee of the Early Childhood Peace Consortium, based in UNICEF (ECPC); Under-Secretary-General of the United Nations (2002–2007)*

"I believe that with Dr. Brown's extensive international experiences in teaching, research, and service, this book will be a great addition to the field of early childhood. With its research-based foundation, this book will be able to aid teachers, early childhood center directors, teacher educators as well as additional key stakeholders to make a better future for children."

Dr. Judit Szente, *University of Central Florida, USA*

"The world is changing more rapidly than ever, and so is early childhood education. Dr. Nancy Brown brings this change to the forefront in this book, helping teachers ensure that all children receive the skills to become aware, adaptable global citizens. This is a must read for teachers who wish to implement changes to their current curriculum that broaden the minds of young children, expand their understanding of others and give them a sense of belonging to today's global community."

Diane Whitehead, *Executive Director of the Association for Childhood Education International, USA*

"Dr. Nancy Brown's book challenges each of us to reach beyond the typical notion of curriculum to one of internationalizing any curriculum to build transformational global competence in children, families, and teachers. Her research and hands-on experiences provide theoretical and practical guidelines to inspire collaborative work in early childhood settings worldwide. This book emphasizes not only curriculum but also the importance of building human relationships, and all early learning advocates should have this information!"

M.J. Steele, *Director of Early Childhood Education for Palm Beach County School District, USA*

Internationalizing Early Childhood Curriculum

Internationalizing Early Childhood Curriculum empowers teachers and directors to internationalize their curriculums around the world in their own unique and culturally specific ways. Serving as a guide and catalyst for thinking about curriculum in our interconnected world, this book explores how young children learn about the world and describes how children develop intercultural understanding, including how their teachers transform to expand their own global awareness and citizenship. Stories from actual classroom curriculum projects are featured, as well as suggested strategies and stages for the process of implementation. Exploring the implications for teacher education and professional development, this book gives readers the tools they need to bring internationalization into their own programs.

Designed to apply to formal and informal early childhood centers across the spectrum, *Internationalizing Early Childhood Curriculum* is essential reading for professional developers and trainers, as well as classroom teachers, directors, policy-makers and NGO professionals providing early childhood services in the U.S. and around the world.

Dr. Nancy Brown is Associate Professor of Early Childhood Education in the College of Education at Florida Atlantic University and serves as Faculty in Residence at the Karen Slattery Educational Research Center for Child Development. For many years she has been a United Nations Representative for the Association for Childhood Education International (ACEI) and has been a long term member of the Committee on Teaching About the United Nations (CTAUN).

Internationalizing Early Childhood Curriculum

Foundations of Global Competence

Nancy Brown

Routledge
Taylor & Francis Group

NEW YORK AND LONDON

First published 2019
by Routledge
52 Vanderbilt Avenue, New York, NY 10017

and by Routledge
2 Park Square, Milton Park, Abingdon, Oxon OX14 4RN

Routledge is an imprint of the Taylor & Francis Group, an informa business

© 2019 Taylor & Francis

The right of Nancy Brown to be identified as author of this work has been asserted by her in accordance with sections 77 and 78 of the Copyright, Designs and Patents Act 1988.

All rights reserved. No part of this book may be reprinted or reproduced or utilized in any form or by any electronic, mechanical, or other means, now known or hereafter invented, including photocopying and recording, or in any information storage or retrieval system, without permission in writing from the publishers.

Trademark notice: Product or corporate names may be trademarks or registered trademarks, and are used only for identification and explanation without intent to infringe.

Library of Congress Cataloging-in-Publication Data
Names: Brown, Nancy, 1951- author.
Title: Internationalizing early childhood curriculum : foundations of global competence / Nancy Brown.
Description: New York, NY : Routledge, 2019. | Includes bibliographical references and index.
Identifiers: LCCN 2018055311 (print) | LCCN 2018059934 (ebook) | ISBN 9781351971560 (eBook) | ISBN 9781138289765 (hardback) | ISBN 9781138289772 (pbk.) | ISBN 9781351971560 (ebk)
Subjects: LCSH: Early childhood education--Curricula. | International education. | Curriculum planning.
Classification: LCC LB1139.4 (ebook) | LCC LB1139.4 .B76 2019 (print) | DDC 372.21--dc23
LC record available at https://lccn.loc.gov/2018055311

ISBN: 978-1-138-28976-5 (hbk)
ISBN: 978-1-138-28977-2 (pbk)
ISBN: 978-1-351-97156-0 (ebk)

Typeset in Sabon
by Taylor & Francis Books

Contents

Acknowledgments

Over the years, I've been fortunate to have outstanding mentors who have guided me along the way, encouraging me, challenging me, and supporting my constant questioning and creative ideas. My mentors helped to make my dreams real, and they were: Mrs. Elsbeth Pfeiffer from Bank Street College of Education, Dr. Leslie Williams and Dr. Maxine Greene from Teachers College, Columbia University, Dr. Laura Ellis and Dr. Joan Bailey from the College of New Rochelle, Mrs. Phyllis Woodbury, an independent educator, and Mr. Gordon Klopf from the World Early Childhood Organization (OMEP) at the United Nations.

I also want to acknowledge my colleagues and friends at Association for Childhood Education International (ACEI), especially Diane Whitehead, Eileen Bayer, and Elisabeth Schuman. Serving as ACEI's United Nations Representative for many years allowed me to interact with people from all around the world, expanding my world view and allowing me to see with new eyes and question in new ways. I am similarly grateful to the Committee on Teaching About the United Nations (CTAUN) for educating me about the world, encouraging me to consider new possibilities in global education, and welcoming my contributions for many years.

For the past 13 years, I have known and worked with the Karen Slattery Educational Research Center for Child Development at Florida Atlantic University. As their curriculum consultant and faculty in residence, I have learned with the teachers about how exciting and energizing early childhood teaching and learning can be. I want to particularly acknowledge my deep appreciation to the director, Lydia Bartram, an unusually gifted leader and colleague, who has allowed me to try out innovations in practice with encouragement and enthusiasm. She supported this book and research from the beginning to its completion. Yoonhee Lee, the graduate research assistant at Slattery, provided extensive and rich classroom observations and insights into the process of internationalization and help in compiling the reference list. Silvana Osorio helped with some of the classroom observations, too. I am grateful to the Global Committee consisting of teachers and the director at Slattery, who collaborated with me on many of the ideological formulations and practical decisions that guided the research and internationalization process. They are: Svetlana Gagula, Sumbla Pervaiz, Consuelo Sheen, Shoshana Hova, Lydia Bartram, and Yoonhee Lee. Their insights and suggestions have been extraordinary and invaluable.

My colleagues in the Department of Curriculum, Culture and Educational Inquiry, in the College of Education at Florida Atlantic University, have strongly supported this project. Department faculty and the Department Chairs, Dr. Emery Hyslop-Margison and Dr. Dilys Schoorman, as well as Dr. Valerie Bristor, the Dean, have been wonderful and supportive. I have learned tremendously over the years from all my undergraduate and graduate students, and especially the doctoral students, and they have helped me to refine my ideas. My students are my inspirations and "bright lights", and they make me feel hopeful in knowing that the current and future generations of young children are in good hands.

Alex Masulis, my editor at Routledge Press, was understanding, thoughtful, patient, and consistently caring in all of our interactions. He encouraged me to identify and reflect upon the universal aspects of everyday life in our school. I am indebted to him and his team, and I thank him for sharing my vision for this book. Many thanks also to the dedicated and exceptionally supportive Misha Kidd, my subsequent editor at Routledge, who enthusiastically guided me through the completion of this manuscript, sharing her expertise and kindness.

My greatest teacher was my mother, Betty Schneider Brown, a leading early childhood educator and pioneer in the field. She was a passionate and brilliant educator. Her love of children and all of humanity guided my life, and my relationship and conversations with her inspired me while I was working on the research for this manuscript. She encouraged authenticity, humility, and innovative thinking. This book is dedicated with profound love and appreciation to her, and her memory is a blessing.

Lastly, and of the absolute utmost importance, is my overwhelming gratitude to the Creator, the Source of All, for the inspiration, courage and Divine Love that animates my life and allows me the great privilege to be of service. My gratitude is boundless and eternal.

Introduction

While I was engaged in the process of researching and writing this book, a four-year-old boy innocently asked a profound and disturbing question, "Why do we have war?" His question stopped me in my tracks and made me reflect on what we were actually doing and why. I remembered why I went into early childhood education: I wanted to contribute to children's lives and to help build the future and make the world a better place. And I thought about how in every generation throughout history, children ask the same question, and yet we continue to go to war. I believe that one child can make a profound difference, and if we could educate young children to embrace one another, learn about and understand each other, and consider themselves citizens of our beautiful and precious planet, maybe we could think about a world at peace. That is why global citizenship and global competence are critically important and, in fact, essential today and every day. As you read this book, I hope that you will experience and realize that in our own individual ways, together with the children, we will create a better world. Let us not lose sight of what is at the heart and soul of early childhood education.

This book will provide a theoretical framework and practical guidelines for internationalizing early childhood curriculum, empowering teachers and directors across the world to internationalize their curriculums in their own unique and culturally specific ways. It is not intended to be a new curriculum model, but rather a way to begin and to continue internationalizing any early childhood curriculum. The book proposes a new vision, raises questions, and encourages educators to consider possibilities for the future of early childhood education around the world. The purpose of the book is to serve as a catalyst and guide for collaborative work among early childhood educators. It has value for private, public, faith-based, NGO-sponsored, family child care, corporate, and all other formal and informal early childhood education centers and settings. Children living in urban and rural areas, in different countries and in different regions of the world can benefit from internationalizing curriculum and learning more about the world. No matter what their economic level or life situation, all young children need to grow up to with an awareness of the world.

I am proposing a way to expand curriculum internationally to promote children's global competence and to support teachers who are developing as global citizens. We will go way "beyond the buzzword" of global citizenship. You will read about everyday projects and activities, including the joys and frustrations of active curriculum development with children. The book provides data from formal and informal research including classroom observations, children's art and writing, parent surveys, classroom observations, and teacher interviews and presentations. This book is designed to explore and illuminate the complexity of days lived with children in their classrooms. It is a practical curriculum book situated right now, in the information age and in the age of globalization of our economy and our future workforce. It is not intended as a "how to" book, but rather a starting point for collaborative work in early childhood schools in different regions of the world. Addressing early childhood educators everywhere, it tells a story and will encourage teachers to discover and create their own stories as they engage in the process of internationalization.

There are five chapters: 1) a rationale, 2) suggested guidelines for the stages of internationalizing early childhood curriculum, 3) stories of the curriculum process in infant/ toddler, three- and four-year-old classrooms, including professional development, 4) "transformational portraits" of the impact on teachers, and 5) a discussion of the conclusions, recommendations, and reflections related to schools everywhere, to formal early childhood teacher education, and to professional development in a variety of school settings. Chapters will conclude with questions for further inquiry that have universal significance and applicability as teachers internationalize their own curriculums in their schools.

I developed a professional development program for teachers at a university-based demonstration preschool and for two years conducted research and data collection specific to classroom practice, teacher's learning processes, and children's perspectives. The third year was designed for the school to function independently, without the researcher. Starting at the beginning of this process, a global committee of teachers and the director in the school thoughtfully supported the process of internationalization. The actual identities of the teachers and children changed over time and their transformations were inspirational. A slow, rich, and complex process lead to increasingly substantive inquiry and continuous curriculum experimentation and exploration. Research documented and undergirded the change process, including accomplishments and challenges that were encountered. The story of internationalizing early childhood curriculum is about the deep and life-changing impact on children, teachers, parents, director, and the entire school community, including the researcher. Early childhood education is a "people business", and what we do depends on our relationships with each other as well as our creativity and commitment to children. The book will emphasize not only curriculum, but the context of human relationships for this transformational process.

Several significant research findings have emerged that have been interesting and relevant for schools everywhere. One finding is that initially I thought I was focusing on global citizenship, but the data revealed that young children are developing the *foundations* of global competence, which will lead to global citizenship. A second important finding, based on ethnographic observational data, was that there were "themes of meaning" that emerged thus through the internationalization of curriculum. They are: 1) an expansion of the experience of community to include the world, 2) the recognition that knowledge is global, 3) helping and making the world better is experienced by children according to their developmental levels, 4) teacher's global citizenship corresponds to what children are taught, 5) family relationships support children's understandings of internationalization and encourage the transfer of knowledge, 6) change is essential for global competence and starts at a young age, and 7) everyone has a different internal cognitive schema of the "world" and these schema can and should be constantly expanded with new educational and interpersonal experiences. These themes are echoed throughout the book, especially in the stories of classrooms that include the children's, teachers', director's and parents' perspectives.

A totally unexpected and major research finding was that teachers were transformed in the development of their own global citizenship, and therefore additional teacher interviews were conducted during the second year of research, demonstrating shifts in the teachers' global awareness, and as they described it, "getting out of their bubble". They talked about going beyond limits and expectations of the children and themselves, and about discovering how much children could understand and do. Additionally, one of the most fascinating ideas that was interwoven through all the data was that knowledge is global and that children, teachers, and parents understand this differently, simultaneously and developmentally. The teachers became more open-minded about learning and about the world. Their inner mental schemas of the world were constantly expanding and being refined. This raises many questions and may add a new dimension in the education of early childhood teachers.

Classroom curriculum projects were surprising and delightful, and although there were some setbacks, the teachers really surpassed all expectations in the first year. The infant and toddler classrooms provide the foundations for global competence at the level of sensory-motor learning. Based on a social constructivist model, the children learn by doing and are developing neurologically, rapidly and with joy. Basic developmental milestones and capacities are being achieved, and these skills prepare the children for the complexities of global competence in years three and four. The foundational aspects of global competence related to developmental theory and best practices are described. The stories of four distinct classrooms of three- and four-year-olds will be recounted and analyzed in greater detail, in terms of the emergent curriculum projects as they were internationalized. The teachers started cautiously, but when their projects were in full swing, the learning was outstanding and innovative.

The first year was the most surprising and indeed ground-breaking for all the classrooms, even though it honestly wasn't easy for many of the teachers. The young three-year-olds worked on an investigation of homes, for people and animals in our community and in the world. They constructed a "home" in the dramatic play area and played on and on, demonstrating increasing levels of social and cognitive development, and they also learned about homes and even bedrooms in other countries. The focus was on homes in the children's families of origin, particularly for children who had been born overseas or whose parents had international backgrounds. The older threes' classroom worked on a project to investigate cities, starting with Boca Raton, where the school is located, and expanding to learn about cities in the world. The children actually visited the local mayor's office, created a voting booth, and constructed a city and an interactive map of our city in the block area. This provided hours and hours of valuable learning through play. Parents and other teachers came into the classroom and shared pictures, stories and artifacts from their cities. This process became interactive and helped children to integrate their learning in meaningful ways. Their classrooms changed and international perspectives were brought into each learning center, and international activities were provided.

The fours' classrooms engaged in projects that lasted throughout the school year, and provided rich, nuanced experiences for children. The children and the teachers seemed to almost never get bored. Developmentally, the children had achieved the language and cognitive skills that allowed them to ask questions, test out their hypotheses, and to spend more time in activities, frequently symbolically representing their advancement in cognitive and neurological development. They drew pictures, created sculptures and structures, and made their own documentation boards, with the teachers' guidance. One classroom of four-year-olds worked on an extensive project about art and architecture around the world, including the Brunelleschi church in Florence, Machu Pichu in Peru, a temple in Korea, and Egyptian pyramids. During this project, the teachers and parents were as engaged as the children. The other four-year-old classroom studied wildlife conservation around the world, creating savannahs, deserts, forests, and other habitats as dioramas made by the children using old pizza boxes. They studied animals such as lions, giraffes, whales and bears one at a time, learning about their lives and needs, and all about endangered species and the environment. This lead them to studying recycling and its impact on the animals. The children made signs and spent a morning actually demonstrating in front of the social science building at the university. Parents participated happily and encouraged their children to have a voice. The children felt quite proud during and after their demonstration, and they talked to university students walking by. There seemed to be no end to the children's investigations about the animals and the environment.

The second year, or "consolidation" year, as it was named, resulted in longer, multifaceted projects on topics such as life under the sea, peace, the rainforest, food, and bees, all topics that generated from the children's interests. The four-year-old children, who had already experienced an internationalized curriculum the previous year, were able to think differently, to see themselves in the world community, and to demonstrate clearly that they were concerned about the problems in the world, and they wanted to take action to make the world a better place. The teachers felt more confident, and collaboration was smoother among colleagues. Generally, the school community felt a sense of accomplishment as the internationalization of the curriculum became familiar and more fully integrated into daily life in the classrooms. The teachers were more willing to take risks and try out new activities and their curriculum decision-making was significantly more autonomous.

The final chapter addresses conclusions, recommendations, and reflections. Some of the recommendations include early childhood teacher education and professional development, from a perspective of teaching and learning "from the inside out" because a teacher's internal schema of the world, and accompanying attitudes and values, significantly impacts on what is taught and experienced by young children. In formal early childhood degree and certification programs, and in ongoing professional development in schools, internationalization, global competence, and global citizenship are addressed as urgent content and process goals. The impact of the United Nations Sustainable Development Goals is paramount and has broad implications for the education of early childhood teachers. New directions for further research, and methods for expanding knowledge are addressed.

We are living in a time of rapid change and global interconnectedness, advances in science and technology, and sadly that also means that we have instant access to global crises, including catastrophic events and violence. Unfortunately, young children may be exposed to the terrorism and hatred in the world, more than we would ever want them to know or experience. We cannot afford to be naïve about situations in the world that may be frightening for our children, and so it is our job to protect them and be intentional about what they learn. They need teachers and parents who make them feel safe and loved every day. We can help them to understand the world better and promote the idea that all over the world there are good people, living productive lives and contributing to humanity in beautiful ways. If we empower young children to feel that they can be proactive and care for others, we have done the children a great service and have supported their strengths and view of their futures. That is the intention of this author. As parents and educators, we, of course, have to monitor what children are hearing and seeing, and do our very best to ensure that our children learn to embrace each other through understanding and compassion for every human being.

Advances in neuroscience substantiate the compelling argument for education in the years from birth to five, because 90 percent of the brain's architecture is developed by five years of age. Technological innovations connect us to the world, more people are crossing borders and demographics are shifting, and it is imperative that we learn to live and work together. I believe that now more than ever, young children need to feel and understand that they belong to a local community, a nation, and to the world. Their construction of knowledge, of their own identities, and of relationships demonstrates the beginnings of their developing global competence.

This book is my offering to you, early childhood teachers everywhere. I have worked in the field of early childhood education for 47 years, as a teacher, center director, dean, and university professor, and I have watched the historical context shift and not shift, sometimes in troubling ways. My Western education requires me to continually stretch and examine my assumptions about the world, and I invite you to join me in this exploration, whoever you are, and wherever you are situated in the world. I am calling for a collective renaissance and reinvigoration of early childhood curriculum theory and practice as teachers, directors, parents and children together create the curriculum of the future. We need a tsunami of love pedagogy through expanding our curriculums to include children and families everywhere in the world. I hope and pray that no child ever again will ask the question, "Why do we have war?"

1 Why International? Why Now?
A Theoretical Rationale

At this moment in history, there is a convergence of ideas and initiatives that point the way to a new and expanded vision for early childhood curriculum, reflecting the content and process of modern life that young children from birth to five years are experiencing. They are literally living in a world where knowledge is transferring across borders because technology and globalization are here to stay and continue to expand exponentially. There is a demand for an increasingly global workforce, and more people are crossing borders than ever before. International policy initiatives, representing collaboration among the global community of nations, have identified educational goals for all the world's children. Advances in neuroscience research have resulted in innovative and more effective instructional strategies, and have demonstrated the indisputable importance of the years from birth to five years. It is time for early childhood curriculum to be reformulated to incorporate 21st-century skills and dispositions. The terms "global citizen" and "global competence" will need to be revisited and refined according to the cultural context of each early childhood setting. Intelligently, deliberately, and honestly, we can internationalize early childhood curriculum and support children in developing the components of global competence that will lead to active and productive global citizenship.

The educational philosopher David Hansen posed the question, "What does it mean to be a teacher in a globalized world?" (Hansen, 2001, p.3). How do we prepare young children for the world of the future? When we reflect on our classrooms and our curriculums, we realize that something has to change, to expand, and to transform. We definitely need self-reflection as well. Are teachers global citizens, too? Early childhood teachers have previously focused on helping young children to become good local and national citizens; now citizenship should include understanding and participating in the local, national, and world communities. We are adding a new dimension to our teaching practice by internationalizing our curriculums and understanding the different factors that are operating in the world and in our profession.

Technology in Context and Shared Knowledge

Early childhood educators are quite aware that young children today live in a very different world than children of past generations. There are economic and political disparities, and children are educated within their specific socio-political and historical contexts, in different countries and regions of the world. Dahlberg, Moss and Pence (1999) describe childhood as a construct that is situated in a range of places, cultures, and times, and that is understood and lived differently depending on class, gender and social and economic conditions. Yvette Murphy (2017) states that interdependence is central in education today, and that teachers play a pivotal role in helping children to understand how they are interconnected with the world. Joel Spring (2015) enumerates four world models of education, including economic, progressive, religious and indigenous models for organizing and implementing curriculum. However, teachers of young children know that no matter what the required model or curriculum regulation, children will be children, and teachers respond to the behaviors and attitudes that young children exhibit in their early childhood classrooms. Globally, Ministries of Education have developed standards for early childhood learning and curriculum, and there are pre-packaged curriculums that claim to be evidence-based and, therefore, valuable and marketable. But something is missing, something has changed, and young children express new understandings and observations of their lived experiences. Their voices are essential, as is their right to know and understand the world around them, regardless of their circumstances. A social constructivist theoretical approach is beneficial because it allows for the active and ongoing creation of local knowledge and a situationally specific, dialogic construction of a world view. Knowledge is now global; it moves around the world. Technology provides a window on the world and the range of content imagery and knowledge is transferred across borders. Early childhood education's content knowledge is transforming, and teachers are watching as children express themselves and learn continuously with excitement and wonder. Young children influence each other as well. Globalization has rigorously and permanently influenced what we and our children define as knowledge, and we are scrambling to keep pace with the onslaught and proliferation of changes.

The availability of technology varies on a continuum from abundance to no access at all, frequently referred to as the "digital divide". In countries where technology is readily available, television and radio bring global information directly into children's homes, and fast-paced and changing technology has become a natural part of children's daily lives. We are definitely living in the information age, with many children exposed to iPads, iPhones, YouTube, Skype, Facebook, and Twitter, apps of all kinds, video games, Google, websites, and online learning activities. Movies designed for young children constitute a lucrative market and are exported around the world. Technology has changed the way young children think about and process knowledge content because in their schools and at home, they are exposed visually to non-present locations and ideas, and time is often compressed. In our classrooms, children engage in dramatic play that demonstrates their exposure to the world through media and through direct travel experiences. They play what they know and they try to make sense of the information they're exposed to. For example, children may view earthquakes, floods, and armed conflict happening all around the world on television, and they openly play and discuss these issues spontaneously in school. Sometimes they see relatives in other countries, and they can even celebrate family celebrations together via Skype. They know there are other countries and that different languages are spoken, although they don't necessarily always comprehend what is being said unless translation is provided.

Children with limited or no access to technology at home may have access in their schools or libraries, perhaps in a restricted fashion. Depending on what forms of technology are being accessed, young children are exposed to imagery and ideas that may or may not match their cultural context. It is possible that in some places young children see images of economically privileged families in other countries and begin to learn consumerist behaviors. In many countries, media is truly reflective of the cultural context and mirrors the population, whether diverse or mono-cultural. Children may learn what is promoted and what comprises the "good life", and they may identify with television characters and/ or national and international heroes. They construct and try to make sense of their worlds through play in blocks, with dolls, through artmaking, and especially in their interactions with other children in communities. Their conversations demonstrate their growing understandings and misunderstandings of the world. In some parts of the world, children and families unfortunately do not have access to technology. However, there are individuals, companies and organizations working toward providing technology and lowering the cost of computers; increased technology access is anticipated and hoped for in the future.

Children often live in neighborhoods that are filled with diverse groups of people, and because of advances of technology, they have greater access to people who live thousands of miles away. Young children are developing rapidly, cognitively and socially, and their understandings of the world are changing every day. Technology is a major influence. Teachers are encouraged to integrate technology into our curriculums, and to the amazement of teachers, young children either know all about iPads, smartphones and apps, and how to use them, or they learn extremely quickly. In his book titled *Technology and Digital Media in the Early Years*, editor Chip Donohue (2015) highlights the importance of developmentally appropriate and intentional use of technology in classrooms with young children and emphasizes the interactive dimension for optimal learning. Technology can be a major tool for internationalizing early childhood curriculum, for helping children to learn that knowledge is global and accessible and that people and ideas are connected all around the world. Technology can be a tool for investigation and research by and for children, and it can be a real window on the world.

The International Community: Global Education First; the Sustainable Development Goals

The international community, comprised of all the countries of the world and generally organized around the United Nations and its agencies, is basically focused on the Universal Declaration of Human Rights, and children's rights in particular. International frameworks and initiatives provide goals and serve as a guide for the world's children, and they are implemented differently in each region and country. In 1990, almost all of the nations of the world dignified and promoted children's rights by signing onto the Convention on the Rights of the Child, ensuring a global process for protecting children's rights. It has been highly successful. Global policies and guidelines sometimes trickle down to the local level, and sometimes they do not. The primacy of local cultures is at best blended "on the ground" with international initiatives which are intended to serve as guideposts for policies and programs.

Mr. Ban Ki-Moon, former Secretary General of the United Nations, in his Global Education First Initiative, identified global citizenship as one of the essential goals for all the world's children (Ban 2012b). This priority was based on the thought that "education must be transformative and bring shared values to life. It must cultivate an active care for the world and for those with whom we share it." To promote global citizenship, we need to "create a generation that values the common good. We must understand how children see the world today – and our schools must foster a broader vision" (Ban 2012b).

Teachers of young children should carefully consider the Secretary General's call for promoting global citizenship because:

- Young children have access to knowledge and to knowledge sharing on a global scale
- Due to the increase in worldwide interactions and relationships, children must learn how to share experiences and communicate with people of different cultural backgrounds
- The skills needed to participate actively in a global world must be practiced early in life, from birth to five years of age, when the brain is developing rapidly
- Young children bring global issues into the classroom
- Our world is interconnected and we are socially, culturally and economically connected
- The future workforce is and will continue to be increasingly global and competitive.

In fall 2015 at the United Nations, after a two-year international collaborative and inclusive process, the countries of the world voted upon and approved the Sustainable Development Goals (SDGs) as guiding global principles for development. This was a ground-breaking event because the

SDGs replaced the former Millennium Development Goals and set goals for the world to achieve by 2030. Education was designated as essential and of central importance, and for the first time, early childhood education was included. Goal Four on quality education is recognized as the driving force for implementation of the other 16 goals because without education, none of the SDGs can be actualized. The significance of the SDGs for teachers, families, children, and all of society cannot be denied. These are positive, life-affirming, and clear goals that will benefit everyone. We are all inter-connected, and so the SDGs all inter-relate and are interdependent. Each goal has sub-goals or targets that further clarify what needs to happen by 2030. The United Nations Sustainable Development Goals (SDGs) are:

- No poverty
- Zero hunger
- Good health and well-being
- Quality education
- Gender equality
- Clean water and sanitation
- Affordable and clean energy
- Decent work and economic growth
- Industry, innovation and infrastructure
- Reduced inequalities
- Sustainable cities and communities
- Responsible consumption and production
- Climate action
- Life below water
- Life on land
- Peace, justice and strong institutions
- Partnerships for the goals.

All the goals impact directly on education and have particular relevance for early childhood curriculum content. It makes sense to address these topics as curriculum projects or themes, at the appropriate developmental level for children from birth to five years. The children in our classrooms today will grow into the adults who will help solve these problems in a very real sense in the world. At a young age, they are learning not only the "what" of curriculum content, but they are also learning the "how" of creative problem solving, essential for the betterment of society. Everyone would benefit if young children started learning about the SDGs at an early age. Descriptions of how this happened in the classrooms in our school will be discussed in Chapter 3 of this book. The SDGs may be integrally related to early childhood curriculum content today and in the future. Early childhood programs anywhere in the world will define their own goals and educational processes, and the international goals of the SDGs and Education First should be debated and discussed in terms of relevance, meaning and cultural specificity.

What is Global Competence and Citizenship for Young Children, Teachers, and Directors?

I have served as United Nations representative for the Association for Childhood Education International (ACEI), and I have participated consistently over the years in the Committee on Teaching About the United Nations (CTAUN). In fall 2013, I attended a participatory meeting of educators where it was stated that young children most likely cannot understand and identify themselves as global citizens until they are nine years old. In my years of classroom teaching and college level teaching, it had become apparent that was absolutely not the case. I currently serve as faculty in residence at an early childhood demonstration school where I have observed young children sharing their developing international awareness, but I never previously called it global citizenship. Based on my work as a teacher and director for many years in a range of early childhood settings in different communities, I know that young children talk about global issues starting with the beginnings of language and social development. That meeting in 2013 was a turning point and wake-up call for me, and I realized that this would be a significant topic for research. I realized that it is important to consciously internationalize curriculum in order for children to become global citizens. And then I had to question further, "What is global citizenship in our classrooms and schools?" What does this really mean? In an age of fast paced globalization and information exchange, is the currently fashionable term "global citizen" merely a new buzzword and rallying point?

The eminent educator John Dewey was particularly concerned with the idea of education for citizenship, and he linked this idea to preparing future citizens in a democracy. Dewey believed that in order for a society to develop citizenry, it had to begin with the education of children (Noddings, 2012, p.37). The concept of "cosmopolitanism", a perspective that regards the world as a focus for citizenship and mutual concern, is not new and has its basis in history. (Noddings, 2012, p.218). Hansen states that cosmopolitanism is an orientation wherein people learn from one another "even while retaining the integrity and continuity of their distinct ways of being." (Hansen, 2011, p.1) The connection of global competence and citizenship with education has been historically integrated into educational systems and their development. Woodrow and Press "advocate for the early childhood institution as a site for the authentic enactment of children's citizenship and a space in which a critical democracy is evident and nurtured" (Woodrow and Press, 2008, p.99). Gaudelli (2016) reminds us that there is no one definition of global citizenship because there are numerous worldviews, inequalities, and purposes for global citizenship education. In our classrooms, we can provide democratic learning activities to ensure that young children learn that they are connected to each other, that they respect and appreciate each other, and that they follow mutually agreed upon rules. However, when we think about and conceptualize the world, what are the undergirding ideas that frame our discourse and understanding? How do we know the world? Where and how is that knowledge created?

Several modern educational theorists have attempted to define global citizenship for children. Margaret Collins includes six aspects of global citizenship: basic needs, environmental issues, fairness, exploring various cultures, democracy, and global issues (Collins, 2008, p.7). Marjorie Ebbeck describes it this way: "We have to build into everything we do with our children the perspective of globalization and the future. Theirs is a new world community and children have to be participants in its planning" (Ebbeck, 2006, p.355). Ebbeck recognizes that children not only respond to the present, but they create the future and they bring their global under- standings to the task. One can therefore conclude that teachers, through their actions in the classroom, actively create the future, too. Yet a clear definition of global citizenship for young children seems elusive.

The question still remains – what characterizes global competence and citizenship for young children? Should we define global identity through the eyes of children only? Alternatively, should we as teachers, struggle together to define these terms in our own ways, in our educational settings? Some of the following ideas may help us think more deeply about these complex concepts.

Three Levels of Identity

Social studies curriculum goals formulated by de Melendez, Beck, and Fletcher (2000, p.9) suggest that young children can develop a triple sense of identity, as follows:

- *Individual identity* – a confident sense of self, family belonging and connection with the cultural background in which the child was brought up
- *National identity* – acknowledgement and pride in the child's country and seeing the self as a citizen of that nation
- *Global identity* – awareness of the world and the self as part of the global community.

Early childhood teachers know that infants and toddlers cannot develop the complex cognitive and social constructs to hold three simultaneous identities. Infants are just beginning to recognize themselves in the mirror and to see themselves as separate from their parents. Toddlers are experi- menting with the sensory properties of their immediate environments, but they can begin to understand videos of places they have never visited. Many toddlers come to school who have already had experiences viewing televi- sion and movies, so they have a visual vocabulary and know the conventions of visual media. However, with intentional teaching and parental support, young children can be guided to organize the sensory data they are exposed to and internally begin to sort it into categories. When they reach the pre- school years, they have a differentiated cognitive capacity and can internalize and express three simultaneous identities, local, national and global. The adults generally understand the word "identity" as similar to "self-concept", which is another way children think about the answer to the ongoing question, "Who am I?" Children may not understand the abstract word "identity", but they will express it in a practical way through their conversations, their play, and their artwork. When children develop the language skills to express their sense of self in community, teachers and parents can expand on their thinking to emphasize and include multiple identities. A child's sense of identity is generally evident whether it is verbally articulated or not.

In his book on cognitive development, David Bjorklund (2012) describes the variability across cultures and the fact that children must have the cognitive skills to adapt to the cultures in which they live. He further states that children across the world are part of a "social species" and they develop the necessary skills to function in their worlds (Bjorklund, 2012, p.439). Young children today are growing up in a global world, and it is necessary for them to develop cognitive and social skills. We also know that young children begin to form their ideas and attitudes about others during the early childhood years. Identity formation is variable and fluctuating, depending on location, gender, race, socio-economic status, and the global awareness of significant adults in children's lives, and the extent that internationalism is integrated in their early childhood curriculums. The three levels of identity present a struggle for young children to integrate into their sense of self in the world. It is an invigorating and realistic struggle, for the children and for their teachers.

Global competence and citizenship are concepts that can be understood and expressed developmentally, for infants and toddlers, preschoolers, and for all people according to their different stages of growth and development. Infants and toddlers are generally developing global competence and four- to five-year-olds are becoming increasingly able to express themselves as global citizens. Examples will be provided later in this book to describe the differences between global competence and global citizenship in the classroom.

It is impossible to compare how adults comprehend global citizenship with the understanding of preschool children. In fact, teachers, parents, and directors are continuously struggling with their identities in a complex and often confusing world. News media provides readily available versions of reality in different countries, and Facebook and other social media allow us to see whatever is posted. It can be challenging to sort out and internally construct an adult schema of the world that we know to be authentic. Global citizenship includes knowledge of the world and the ability or agency to take action to make the world a better place. Adults who consider themselves global citizens would not only know about the world and the inequities, but they would know how to advocate and make changes to solve and resolve global and local problems. The truth is that we are all learning from multiple sources about the world, and this impacts on our identity development significantly. Adults today are struggling with our own inner narratives and our multi-faceted identities.

Three Essential Aspects of Global Competence and Citizenship for Young Children

The foundation for global competence can be built into the early childhood curriculum. Corresponding with each child's developmental level, I believe that global competence is comprised of the following elements which will be explored in this book:

- *Children becoming global citizens who have real content knowledge about the world*
- *Children developing the skills and dispositions needed for communication, relationship building, collaborative problem solving, and creative thinking*

Global citizenship can similarly be intentionally embedded in the early childhood curriculum, usually for children around four years of age but possibly earlier, and includes the following:

- *Children becoming aware, able and eager to engage in service to the world community*

The Changing World and 21st-Century Skills

Ministries of Education have increasingly designated early childhood learning standards in their national education policies and agendas. Global awareness, along with multiple language learning, is frequently included because countries are recognizing the benefits for participation in the global economy. In some instances, economic factors have driven the choice to include the global dimension, while in other countries, the humanitarian principles of human rights and international understanding and peace are the underlying reasons. Western notions of education have dominated, and colonization has unfortunately stifled the voices of many but not all indigenous people. Thankfully, that is changing. In the world, voices are being raised and educational policies are shifting, but violence and war, food insecurity, and other forms of inequity unfortunately and sadly prevail. The principle of the "preservation of privilege" tends to limit free expression and human rights. At the risk of sounding naïve and far too idealistic, I believe that the dichotomies of Western and non-Western, rich and poor, North and South, and that kind of dualistic thinking, should not drive our thinking or our educational systems. People and life circumstances are complex, and we can't understand if we oversimplify with stereotypes and categories. Rather, I keep my focus on young children and the gifts each one of them brings into our world, and my intention is to enrich early childhood curriculum to integrate the world into our children's consciousness and to help them move the world forward and make it a better place.

The United States Department of Education created an International Strategy for 2012–2016 titled *Succeeding Globally through International Education and Engagement* (2012). Former Secretary Arne Duncan stated in 2011, "We must focus on integrating international perspectives into our classrooms. It is through education and exchange that we become better collaborators, competitors and compassionate neighbors in this global society" (Duncan, 2011). This is a major step forward. Four priorities have been identified by the U.S. Department of Education:

- Global competencies for all students
- A world-class education for all students
- International benchmarking and applying lessons learned from other countries
- Education diplomacy and engagement with other countries.

In the information age, life happens differently, and people are discovering and practicing new ways of interacting. Although human relationships are and will remain fundamentally interpersonal, adults and some children's interactions now are specifically online. People are texting, Facetiming and Skyping, and the use of social media is rampant. Definitions of "friends" are changing. Young children who have technology available have access to knowledge from all around the world; they need to learn how to use that knowledge creatively and for the greater good. That means they need to develop collaborative problem-solving skills and creativity in order to meet the challenges of the information age. They need to learn to ask important questions. The global village is here and now. We will not go back to the old way of thinking. Costa and Kallick comment that "our students are in the 21st century, and they are waiting for the teachers and the curriculum to catch up" (Costa and Kallick, 2010, p.211) What does that mean for the classroom teacher?

Television and websites provide young children with global news, with stories that are uplifting and many that are upsetting and violent. Young children in the early childhood years readily absorb these images. Their concepts of community are changing, as are their cognitive processes. They are aware earlier of non-present reality and their sense of sequential time is variable. Children learn the difference between real time and online experiences. They are aware of different countries, different languages, and different holiday celebrations. As previously mentioned, some children in wealthier neighborhoods have smartphones and can access people and knowledge with a click. Other young children are sadly left out of the information age, in varying degrees, due to the digital divide that separates the rich and the poor and denies access to technology to poor children. This is, indeed, an extremely serious problem.

An internationalized curriculum is a necessity, and change is happening every day. The new wording is "21st century skills" for the information age.

Heidi Hayes Jacobs addresses the issue in her book titled *Curriculum 21: Essential Education for a Changing World* (2010). She explains that classrooms can be aligned with schoolwide, community, national and, in fact, global perspectives, stating that the "ultimate zoom in is the individual child" (Hayes Jacobs, 2010, p.21). The interconnectedness of human life, ideas, and products are evident as the global economy changes and expands on the internet. Economic markets have become global, resulting in a globalized economy. Eminent scholar Dr. James Banks has recently added a sixth stage to his typology of the stages of cultural identity, defined as globalism and global competency. (Banks, 2016, p.174). Internationalization is recognized as central in education. Virtual reality and holographs will be developed further and available in the future, along with innovative technologies that have yet to be invented.

Author and visionary Tony Wagner has written about the survival skills that children will need in what he defines as the "new world of work". These skills include:

- Critical thinking and problem solving
- Collaboration, agility and adaptability
- Initiative and entrepreneurialism
- Effective written and oral communication
- Accessing and analyzing information
- Curiosity and imagination. (Wagner, 2010, p.15–41)

These skills are and will be experienced by young children, depending on their developmental levels, educational environments, and family systems. These skills apply to what children need to do with knowledge, how they can interact with ideas and facts, and how they can do this in a social context. That is why an international approach that is experiential is needed in their education.

The Partnership for 21st Century Learning has added more skills they believe will be needed:

- Creativity and Innovation
- Critical thinking and problem solving
- Communication
- Collaboration
- Information literacy
- Media literacy
- ICT (Information, Communications and Technology) literacy
- Flexibility and adaptability
- Social and cross-cultural skills(Battelle for Kids, 2019)

The speed of change and the lists of skills needed for future success can be overwhelming and daunting for a classroom teacher. In early childhood, we have traditionally emphasized content areas such as math, science, reading, art, and music. However, if we re-examine our view of the future, we recognize that it can be positive and uplifting. The classroom teacher is challenged to teach for the joy of learning now, in the moment, and for preparing young children for an unpredictable and expanding future.

Daniel Pink reminds us that we are entering a new age that encourages the right-brain qualities of inventiveness, empathy, joyfulness, and meaning, qualities that are positive and life-affirming and can serve to energize or view of the future. His approach is hopeful, and he invites us to enter the new landscape of the "six senses" which he identifies as design, story, symphony, empathy, play and meaning (Pink, 2006, p.3–4). That sounds a little more inviting, even though it doesn't exactly sound like the learning standards that many of us are accustomed to, or the early childhood quality indicators that we have been educated to incorporate into our classroom curriculums. Pink's thinking provides us with an easier starting point, an entry into more humanistic concepts as we endeavor to internationalize our curriculums to bring our children into the 21st century.

How we prepare young children for the future workplace additionally involves sensitivity to others and the ability to communicate across cultures. The numbers of people who are immigrating within and across countries are increasing every day. In large urban centers especially, diversity of all kinds is increasing. It is predicted that within the next decade, more and more people will be living in big cities all around the world, and in many instances, this is already the case. Family structures are changing and the idea of a traditional family unit has been replaced by the option to live in a variety of family constellations. Multiple languages are needed in order to communicate with people in different regions, and in many of our classrooms today. The work-force of the future demands not only an international perspective, but the linguistic skills to communicate across cultures, too.

Based on what we know today about the information age, the shifting global economic system and the future workforce, we can make an educated guess about what 21st century skills will be needed. But one thing is for sure, children will need to be able to adapt to change readily, and to respond to change with creativity, innovation, collaboration, and compassion. Children will have to see themselves not only as responders, but as the creators of positive change and initiators of a better future.

Early Childhood Curriculum: Current Issues and Future Perspectives

Curriculum is the key to early childhood education. There is nothing more important or more meaningful than what happens every day in our class-rooms. The intellectual and social environment of the classroom is what children internalize as their model of life in a community. When they leave our preschools and enter kindergarten in more formal settings, they take the model of what they've learned with them on the inside. Early childhood education really happens inside the child, because the child's mind is the center of integrated knowledge. The child takes with her or him the gifts of social and emotional development, cognitive skills, and enthusiasm for life and learning. The child similarly carries within a view of the self in the world that was demonstrated and lived in his or her classroom. That is why, at this time in history, young children need to develop the three essential elements of global competence and citizenship and three levels of identity as an individual, a citizen of the nation, and a citizen of the world. Every child in the world deserves to know that he or she is part of the world, and this should be a right, not an option.

Therefore, internationalizing early childhood curriculum becomes essential. We do not lose anything, but rather we add on and blend in a global sense of reality into our classrooms. Children around the world may be receiving television images and social media images in their homes that often reflect increasing violence, terrorism, plane crashes, natural disasters, and wars, resulting in a frightening and distorted view of people in the world. Early childhood curriculum needs to provide an alternative, life affirming view of people living in other countries and the beauty of their daily lives, rather than the negativity. Our classrooms need to give children a sense that there is good news in the world, and that there are people engaged in positive activities together. Can we empower children to explore and continuously learn about the world in an authentic way that helps them create meaning about the global nature of knowledge and about relationships across borders?

Curriculum Models with an International Perspective

No one understood better than Maria Montessori how important it was and is for young children to learn about the world. Historically, she was probably the first early childhood educator who brought global activities into the curriculum she designed. She believed that young children should learn about the different countries in the world through direct experiences. Montessori schools are in operation in many countries around the world, and her ideas have been adapted to the specific locations. The overarching ideas that Maria Montessori contributed were related to global learning through education for peace. She felt that classrooms were places where children could learn and rehearse conflict negotiation and resolution strategies (Duckworth, 2006, p.39). Montessori believed that young children were pure and able to learn about peace, and that the foundations for peace could effectively be established in the early childhood years.

Montessori additionally included the concept of map making and geography so that children could see and understand the difference between countries and the globe. Routines and daily activities were times when a global view could be infused into the curriculum. For example, in a Montessori school in Washington, D.C., the curriculum includes an international snack day where children bring in snacks, costumes, and stories from different countries. Some schools have instituted a peace table or peace rug in the classroom, as a designated place for children to practice conflict resolution. Peace assemblies are also part of the curriculum in these schools (Duckworth, 2006, p.44–47). In each country where Montessori schools exist, the Montessori global aspect of early childhood curriculum has been blended with the religious and cultural beliefs of the country. Peace and international mindedness is respected and expected, and is often the center of discussion among teachers, parents and children.

Another well-known early childhood curriculum based on the principles of preparing children for global citizenship is the *International Baccalaureate (IB) Primary Years Programme*. The IB curriculum is widely utilized in the international school system around the world and has been used in some public and private schools as well. The IB curriculum has the following "transdisciplinary" goals for children to learn:

- Who we are – the self, what it means to be human
- Where we are in place and time – inquiry about place in history and interconnectedness
- How we express ourselves – discovering and expressing ideas, aesthetics, values and creativity
- How the world works –inquiry into the natural world, science, technology and the environment
- How we organize ourselves –interconnectedness of people, organizations, communities
- Sharing the planet – sustainability, rights, peace, conflict resolution, access to resources

(International Baccalaureate, 2014)

The IB Primary Years Programme includes the early childhood years, and it is basically a constructivist, inquiry-based approach with a central focus on educating the global citizen. According to George Walker, the former IB director general, the IB curriculum is designed in stages to first give children an understanding of international awareness, then global awareness, and then they are expected to embody the notion of global citizenship, which the IB states includes rights and privileges. They believe that action and active engagement are essential for children to consider themselves to be global citizens (Walker, 2010). The actual content of the curriculum supports and promotes global competence and citizenship, along with high academic performance expectations even in the early years. In the IB curriculum, it is recognized that global citizenship is based on the fusion of pedagogy, concepts, skills and attitudes. They define success by measuring student action in wanting to make the world a better place (Davy, 2011, p.9). Their mission statement emphasizes "that the IB nurture a culture that is creative, alert and flexible. Educating for the 21st century is an exciting and urgent responsibility. Our collective future depends on it" (Davy, 2011, p.10).

The *International Step by Step Association* (ISSA), in its publication *Competent Educators of the 21st Century* , defines its vision as, "With support from family and community, every child reaches his or her full potential and develops skills necessary for being successful and active members of a democratic knowledge society" (ISSA, 2010). The Step by Step curriculum principles of democratic participation includes making choices, taking initiative, valuing individual expression, and contributing as a member of a learning community. This curriculum includes many of the child-centered concepts that are accepted today as early childhood quality indicators. The Step by Step curriculum has been implemented primarily in the European countries and it is understood as a way to lay the foundation for future citizenship in a democracy.

Montessori, International Baccalaureate, and Step by Step are examples of some curriculum models with a global vision, and there are many more. In some countries, spiritual and religious values with global ideals are integrated into the early childhood national learning standards. Each model contributes to our knowledge about international early childhood curriculum, however, no one curriculum model has all the answers. All early childhood models can be internationalized, and the foundations of global competence can be creatively developed. Goals for early childhood global education have been suggested by Bell, Jean-Sigur and Kim (2015), such as perspective consciousness, cross-cultural awareness, state-of-the-planet awareness, system connectedness, awareness and utilization of technology, and options for participation. However, every early childhood center will discover and identify their own global goals and activities, and these will probably change depending on the children's and teacher's learning. Chapter 2 of this book provides suggested guidelines for this process. Group discussions and brainstorming sessions among early childhood teachers and directors in their respective schools are expected to be extremely rich and productive. Our creativity and inspired vision can be applied to how well we can educate our children in early childhood centers in culturally unique settings, in different countries in the world. In the future, the global dimension will become the "new normal".

Learning Standards, Professional Organization Frameworks, and Goals

International early childhood curriculum, which includes global competence and citizenship for children, is guided by national standards and goals in different ways. The actual implementation of standards and how they are used is variable; however it important to focus on specific standards in order to understand, justify and promote innovation and curriculum change. At the heart of all the standards is the notion of children as productive members of community. Early childhood education learning standards are established in national Ministries of Education, and are also written and utilized by non-governmental organizations that sponsor early childhood programs for children, some region-specific and some country-specific. There are corporate, for profit organizations that are designing and promoting early childhood education, and these programs and their goals are being marketed to countries. Faith based early childhood programs have religious and other standards and goals for young children. Not all learning standards reflect a global perspective, but there is potential for this to happen, as is the intention of this research and book.

The curriculum position statement conceptualized and developed in the United States, "Developmentally Appropriate Practice" (DAP) from the National Association for the Education of Young Children (NAEYC) emphasizes "creating a caring community of learners" as a major goal. Community is described as a place where children feel safe and valued, and is "conducive to the learning and well-being of all" (Copple and Bredecamp, 2009, p.16). Understanding of cultural differences and appreciating others, stated clearly in DAP, relates to international early childhood curriculum because the idea of community is extended to include local, national and international levels of community. If young children learn about how we are interconnected, then their experience of community is larger and more inclusive. Their experience of community can embrace other countries, too, and therefore the world. NAEYC has initiated a global department in its organization, with professional connections, networks and collaborations. NAEYC significantly includes notions of culture, community, and outreach that have global implications.

In 1999, the Association for Childhood Education International (ACEI) and the World Early Childhood Organization (OMEP) were collaborators and pioneers in producing the *Early Childhood Education and Care in the 21st Century: Global Guidelines*, outlining an international perspective for all aspects of early childhood education. The guidelines subsequently have been researched by ACEI in many countries, and proven to be meaningful and relevant. Additionally ACEI has initiated a Global Schools First accreditation program that includes certification in global education. ACEI utilizes a whole school approach to global education and affirms that "a globalized world requires education that empowers learners to value national, social, racial, cultural and religious differences while embracing our common humanity" (www.acei.org). To support and strengthen national early leaning standards and guidelines, the World Early Childhood Organization (OMEP) has regional and country professional early childhood networks; and the World Forum on Early Care and Education, another international early childhood professional organization, similarly convenes global conferences and promotes publications and global sharing of ideas and standards for quality early childhood practice.

The National Council for the Social Studies (NCCS), a professional organization based in the United States, has published national standards intended to prepare children with the skills, knowledge and dispositions to participate in an active life as future citizens. Recognizing the impact of globalization and advances in technology, NCSS standards emphasize civic engagement and the development of the process of what it takes to be an informed and competent citizen in a democratic society (National Council for the Social Studies, 2013).

The NCSS Curriculum Standards include ten themes, and seven of these themes are particularly relevant for the early childhood years. They are

- *Culture* – cultural diversity and multicultural topics in the curriculum
- *Time, continuity and change* – for young children, learning about time sequences and how there is a past, present and future; that change is a natural process to be expected, and developing skills for adapting to change
- *People, places and environments* – mapping and geographical skills and concept development, how things work and where resources come from, how environments differ across the world
- *Individual development and identity* – personal identity and how it is shaped, characteristics of identity
- *Global connections* – connections between people, products, and natural environments
- *Civic ideals and practices* – principles of democratic society, including majority rule, respect for differences, shared decision-making

(National Council for the Social Studies, 2014)

The Partnership for 21st Century Skills has published *The P12 Common Core Toolkit: A Guide to Aligning the Common Core Standards with the Framework for 21st Century Skills* (2014). Designed to build unified curriculum goals, the future-oriented 21st century skills support common core goals of English language arts and mathematics. This includes core content mastery combined with collaboration, critical thinking and problem solving, innovation and creativity. One of the key areas of alignment that relates to international early childhood curriculum is global awareness and the understanding of other perspectives and cultures. Both the common core and the 21st century skills similarly promote interpersonal communication, especially speaking and listening, as essential for problem solving and reasoning. Information literacy and technology are emphasized as well, both leading to a global perspective, and both helping children to build a strong knowledge base. International early childhood education lays the foundation for future success in the common core curriculum that many young children encounter in K-12 schools in the United States, and in curriculums designed for other nations and regions of the world. By enhancing social and intellectual development, young children will be able to meet the learning standards and to embody the 21st century skills in their school careers and in the future workforce.

In many countries in the world, national governments, in their Ministries of Education, have established early childhood national curriculum standards. Depending on the cultural, social and religious nature of each different society, the standards have been formulated to promote national citizenship and to strengthen the future of each nation. International early childhood education does not mean that national citizenship is ignored or that loyalty to one's nation should not be important. Internationalizing curriculum means that we educate young children to be citizens of their nations and of the world at the same time. We "add on" global learning but we do not throw away what is already meaningful and relevant to each country's national goals.

International organizations have taken a central and innovative role in providing international connections so that children understand that they are interrelated to other people in the world. One example is a global, collaborative initiative sponsored by UNICEF titled "Peacebuilding through Early Childhood Development", and its partners are international. The conceptual framework identifies early childhood development as an agent for change and community development, particularly in developing countries. Yale Child Study Center has partnered with UNICEF to co-lead this project, and to set the goals and activities that are changing communities and working diligently to build more peaceful societies. It is not a curriculum initiative; however, the intention is to work around the world and share knowledge across borders, among partner communities. An interdisciplinary, multisector approach leverages the potential of communities and provide for young children's development. The theme of expanded communities correlates with an international approach to early childhood curriculum because young children's learning starts local and then becomes global.

Another example is the ATD Fourth World Movement, an NGO that works in communities with young children and their families who are living in poverty around the world. Inspired by its founder, Joseph Wresinski, the goal is to empower and dignify poor communities by creating street libraries with and for children. Their stories are written down and then shared around the world with children in different countries through a program called Tapori. Although it is not a formal early childhood school, informal community locations educate young children about children in other nations by living together in communities. The children learn that they are part of the global community and they are not alone. UNICEF and the ATD Fourth World Movement are examples of organizations providing informal, innovative international educational perspectives for children in the early childhood years.

What Can We Do?

We are at a critical juncture in history, with the Sustainable Development Goals, Education First Initiative, and the 21st century skills movement. Technology is here to stay and has significantly changed our lives. Increasing technological advances are anticipated that could additionally alter the way we educate our children. If young children, their teachers and directors, and their parents could collaborate to produce and experience internationalized curriculums, the future might look very different. If young children could understand how people really live around the world, they would grow up to create a peaceful world and they would share with one another. Maybe that is what early childhood education is all about. That would mean that as teachers, we would need to transform our identities and see ourselves as global citizens so we could help children learn internationally. Children would be prepared differently and more effectively for an uncertain and challenging future workforce. We would need to think simultaneously about our local, national, and global world. We are on the forefront of creating something new, and that means taking risks and experimenting, and acknowledging that knowledge is global and our curriculums are, too. We wouldn't lose our other goals for quality early childhood education, like for example literacy skills and mathematical thinking; rather, we would add on and expand how and what we teach – the foundations of global competence and global citizenship.

There is nothing more powerful, more life changing, and more profound than the presence of a great teacher in an early childhood classroom and in a school, or in an informal community early childhood setting. Teachers and supportive directors are the driving force and the catalyst to make authentic curriculum happen. John Dewey said that using one's mind creatively when engaging in curriculum development and that act of testing out one's ideas was real intellectual freedom (Tanner, 1997, p.69). It is the job of teachers today to claim and express that intellectual freedom. Maria Acevedo recently wrote about intercultural understanding for young children, stating that it is important because it helps "to transform our global society in to a just and equitable world" (Acevedo, 2016, p.42)

As educators and learners, it is time to pause and reflect on our teaching practice and on who we are. One of my insightful and kind former professors, Harriet Cuffaro, wrote that:

> Teaching is a way of being who we are and a place where in our actions we make manifest what we believe and value. Teaching is a way of rehearsing and trying identity, of creating and discovering self. In teaching, self is constantly elicited, always on call, responding. There is an alertness required, an alertness to understand each situation, the meaning and possibilities of the present moment, an alertness that throws us back to self, to reason-making.
>
> (Cuffaro, 1995, p.99)

I invite you on this journey. In the next chapter, you will be introduced to the Slattery Center, and the story of how teachers and a director in one courageous school struggled to internationalize their early childhood curriculum. There are many ways to proceed with this process, and some guidelines will be suggested to support you. I hope you'll feel empowered to create an international early childhood story of your own, wherever you are. The world is changing and so must we.

Questions for Further Exploration

1   Am I ready to internationalize my curriculum? What should I do to get ready?

2   Can knowledge be local and shared globally? How might that happen in my school?

3   How might I use technology to enrich international learning and global competence and citizenship for young children?

4   In what ways could the Sustainable Development Goals (SDGs) be addressed in the content of my early childhood curriculum themes, activities and projects?

5   How am I a global citizen and a citizen of my country? How might I become more globally competent so I can educate the children about the world? How can I gain more authentic and meaningful knowledge about the world?

6   What do the children in my class know about the world? How do they know this? Where did they get this information?

7   In an age of increasing violence and terrorism, especially in the media, would a global perspective on curriculum shift societal consciousness to international understanding and promote peace? Do I believe that peace on earth could be a reality, and that education might help to actualize this ideal?

8   Can I work within my own school, within the school's policies, limitations and expectations, and embrace the freedom to make changes and create something new? Can I find a way to initiate and work with other teachers and the director to internationalize our early childhood curriculum?

9   Am I open to experience the inevitable transformation and growth that I will experience? Do I have the courage to grow and learn?

2 Guidelines for Internationalizing Early Childhood Curriculum

"Going global" in early childhood curriculum implies a deeper under-standing of all aspects of curriculum and the development of children's skills and dispositions to further learning and growth in an interconnected world. Global citizenship education has become fashionable and words like "global child", "global classroom", and "global competence" have become terms that educators use interchangeably and, frequently, superficially. That's because there is no one way to educate children about the world, and there are few benchmarks or guidelines to determine how this can actually be developed and achieved. Internationalizing early childhood curriculum is clearly not the absolutely ultimate way to educate the future generation, but it is a very significant piece of the educational jigsaw puzzle that con-tinuously adapts and responds to societal trends and shifts. An obvious and somewhat shocking omission in the research and literature on inter-nationalization has been in the field of early childhood curriculum. When and how global education starts and develops is critically significant and implies a process of curriculum change. Although the field of early child-hood education has made advances in quality curriculum, and in multi-cultural education and social studies, the international dimension currently deserves our professional attention. Making change in a school is easier said than done. It is at best a planned process that proceeds according to the defined and expected goals. In a practical sense, it is a messy and somewhat unpredictable endeavor requiring patience, persistence and courage in the face of uncertainty. It is a schoolwide learning process that involves and impacts on everyone, including teachers, the director, parents and children. There is no "one size fits all" recipe for success.

The multi-year research and curriculum development process at the Karen Slattery Educational Research Center for Child Development (Slattery) unexpectedly led to the emergence of stages of the process of internationalization which I hope will serve as guidelines and catalysts for other schools to internationalize their own curriculums. This was a great surprise. We never intended to produce stages for implementation; these stages became apparent as our research process developed. The research was qualitative, with multiple data collection methods that were ongoing, and with initial IRB approval from the university; however, several new and exciting data collection methods emerged. It became clear that both formal and informal research methods would give us the best data to help us understand what the foundations of global competence are. I conceptualized this research project as an art form; the fine art of creative investigation. In the second year of the project, the original research questions about global citizenship were refined to address global competence in children and global citizenship for teachers and the director. A more detailed description of the research process and findings will be provided in Chapters 3 and 4. One truth became obvious and evident: we were all learning and our lives were transforming, including myself. As a school, we engaged deeply in the process and worked diligently for those three pivotal years. Much of what we learned has become a part of who we are today. The "how to" has become demystified by the designation of stages for internationalization of early childhood curriculum.

Although Slattery is a demonstration school, we experience what early childhood schools address in any setting, including and not limited to the "who, what, when, where and how" of early childhood education. Teachers and directors everywhere are concerned about child development, what we teach and how we teach in terms of quality curriculum and activities, scheduling, assessment and evaluation of children's learning and teacher performance, and professional development regarding how we grow and continue to learn as teachers. Other universal issues include discovering, gathering and inventing resources, and the impact of location, culture, sociopolitical factors and budgets on what curriculum we can provide.

At Slattery, we are challenged with those very basic considerations and curriculum components daily. We are not specifically a model program per se, but rather a focal point for investigation and innovation in early childhood education. We ask a lot of questions and continually evolve and refine our work with young children.

The following sections present four stages of internationalization, beginning with a description of the stage, and then providing a practical explanation and synopsis of our process at Slattery. A set of questions for further investigation are provided to help educators apply and think through some of the issues that we encountered and how site-specific applications can be formulated. Early childhood schools are encouraged to define and refine their own process accordingly. You are also encouraged to ask new questions and to go beyond what worked in our school. In that way, we all benefit and learn, and true internationalization can become a global early childhood education phenomenon.

Stage One: Planning

Planning is generally designed to be a logical process, with built-in opportunities for flexibility, refinement and revisiting what works. Unforeseen changes will inevitably be made as the process unfolds. However, the planning process should start with a comprehensive understanding and articulation of the characteristics of your unique school setting, and the geographical location with its benefits and challenges. Curriculum mandates and regulations and all accreditation documents should be reviewed to determine if global curriculum content is expected and required, and if so, how "global" is defined. The curriculum is a leverage point for inserting global content throughout the process of play, conversations, activities and community involvement. Depending on your curriculum model, you may be able to build in global learning or change or delete other outdated content, if necessary. The population of children should be inventoried to assess how many normally developing children there are, how many children with atypical development and how many are from different countries and are dual language learners. These factors must be part of the planning stage as you determine what kinds of special supports may be needed and if the anticipated supports are available and possible as you plan to change and expand your curriculum.

Before internationalizing the curriculum, a school needs to know itself, to define itself and to write, create and/ or review its philosophical principles. The decision to make change and to internationalize is a big one, requiring additional work, learning and courage. It can be both exhilarating and discouraging at times. The school should start with a clear self-definition and move forward continuously from there. Hopefully the decision to internationalize will be a collective decision, but in many settings, the decision may be made by the director and other administrators, or in a school district, company or non-profit organization.

It is necessary to identify how curriculum change will take place in your school. The director's role is crucial as a major change agent for the support and implementation of the internationalization process. Professional development opportunities for the teachers can stimulate change, therefore it helps to define what professional development time will be allocated. For deep, thoughtful change to take place, a two- to three-year period would be optimal, and time needs to be allocated for daily or weekly curriculum planning. In every school, change takes place differently, on a continuum from more directed change to more autonomous change and varying levels of teacher empowerment. It is helpful to think through exactly how you anticipate change would happen in your school and what the desired outcomes might be. Think about what you would do when something doesn't go smoothly or when the natural obstacles of life with young children get in the way, such as children with colds who are absent, teacher turnover, family crises, weather conditions that impact on attendance, staff dynamics and teaching teams that are functioning with varying degree of effectiveness. Change can be accelerated by teachers who constantly want to please the director, and cooperation or resistance can occur, depending on the teacher's own personality and the relationship with the director. Competition, instead of collaboration, and general confusion also may be evident in daily life in a school. Defining and outlining the change process in your school would be helpful. Any supportive structures you can provide would further enhance the change and expansion process. The director need not be the only one who is a change agent or who tracks and encourages change. Everyone should clearly understand what roles they play in the internationalization process in your school.

Formal and informal evaluation and assessment happens in almost every school. Planning for evaluation implies that there is a goal, even if no one knows exactly what the outcome will look like. Some schools identify concrete goals, and others are comfortable with more process-oriented goals such as exploration and investigation. Your school will need to identify how you know you've been successful, and how you define success, for both the process and the end product. How does assessment of curriculum occur in general in your school, and how might that be tweaked to address the international dimension of education? How might you determine if individual teachers are successful, and how would you be sure if the whole school was working together as a team to achieve the goals? It would be important to let teachers know in advance how they are being evaluated. The role of evaluation should be revisited, too, especially if evaluation is the criteria for teachers retaining their jobs. In all instances, if teachers know in advance what is expected, they will have a sense of security that will guide their learning and curriculum building process. It is certainly acceptable and perhaps optimal to let everyone know that making mistakes is a learning process, and that assessment, whether formative or summative, is intended to be supportive and instructional, not punitive. Change is influenced by culture, locale and type of school, available global resources and the personalities of the teachers and director play a central role in how curriculum develops and is implemented.

The Process at Slattery

I have served as faculty in residence, curriculum consultant and researcher at Slattery for many years. For the purposes of this research and discussions of ongoing daily operations, I refer to Slattery as a school, not a preschool. We are not "pre" anything; we are a school educating young children from six months to five years of age. I initiated and implemented a multi-year research process at Slattery, to investigate how children become global citizens and how the foundations of global competence can be achieved in our classrooms and schools. I had no idea how complicated this process would be when we were engaged in the planning stage.

Slattery is located in South Florida, in the United States, on the campus of a large public university, and we are affiliated with the College of Education. Our population consists of 100 children and is definitely multicultural, with children from all around the world, many of whom speak different languages. We are considered a private school serving the university community of students, staff, and faculty and basically, the population is middle class and pays tuition, except for four-year-olds who receive a funding subsidy from the state. We have a limited budget for classroom supplies although we realistically make and invent most of our own learning materials. Slattery uses a project-based, eclectic curriculum, and we are accredited locally and nationally. We follow state mandates for demonstration lab schools on university campuses. Slattery teachers, like the children, come from different countries and are able to follow a cohesive and progressive curriculum philosophy centered on project-based learning. We provide six staff development training days per year for all the teaching staff. The teachers are an extremely dedicated professional group who take great pride in their work. There are six lead teachers and six assistant teachers, with additional assistants in each classroom depending on the age of the children. We follow the staffing ratios set forth in our national accreditation standards from NAEYC. There is one director, two administrative assistants and one faculty in residence.

At Slattery, we emphasize and celebrate the principles of creativity, transformation and service to humanity. These principles apply to the children, teachers, parents and the director, the entire learning community. Over the years, through continuing staff development and mentoring of staff, we together formulated core values which undergird our teaching and learning, as follows:

1 Education takes place in love. Without love there is no education and no learning.
2 Teachers are professionals who consciously create curriculum, not mere implementers of a prescribed curriculum.
3 The creativity of teachers and children is central to all we do.
4 Everyone is learning; we are a learning community.
5 Children learn neurologically in an integrated way, so curriculum must be integrated for optimal learning.
6 Keep everyone excited and enthusiastic about learning.
7 Build on the strengths of teachers and children, honoring their differences in multiple intelligences and interests.
8 Knowledge is co-constructed, not transmitted. Knowledge is fluid and changes in the context of relationships and activities.
9 Leadership is collaborative and dialogic, and non-punitive. The director's role is supportive and relational.
10 Technology is integrated into curriculum projects, and interactive whenever possible; technology is not a separate subject.
11 The environment is a teacher. We intentionally change our environments to promote children's learning.
12 Spanish is a second language taught in our curriculum; however, we are not a bilingual program.
13 We start with a project-based learning environment; however, we are essentially eclectic, incorporating the best of all the different curriculum approaches to support children's learning.

14   Curriculum activities take place indoors and outdoors; connections with nature are encouraged.
15   We are open to change and we listen carefully to the voices of the children.

There are several ways we seek to achieve change in our curriculum, but at first we were honestly puzzled about how to think about the change process. I had returned from Malaysia with the director and we were looking at Slattery in light of our visit to early childhood centers in Kuala Lumpur. That was a catalyst for beginning discussions between the director and myself. Typically we planned our staff development days collaboratively, and this time we began to incorporate a larger vision, starting with a plan to show a video about babies around the world and an analysis of how children are influenced by their cultures, in general, and families. We agreed that professional development would be key to enriching the perspectives of the staff, and I began thinking about how research should be embedded in the process, although I wasn't sure at all what that might look like or what the research questions would be.

The staff development training days were my responsibility to design and teach, with the supportive and collaborative input from the director. That spring a staff development day addressed the topic of exploring and understanding culture in the context of early childhood curriculum. We examined and tried to understand the relationship between children, culture, family and curriculum. Teachers were asked to reflect on how their own cultural backgrounds affected them, and we discussed the idea of cultural identity, which is integral to early childhood education and a hot topic for teachers. There was confusion about what constituted culture, and what defined race, country of origin, economic class, religion, country of citizenship, and country of residence. We examined data from our population, with numbers of children from different countries and who spoke languages other than English, the primary language in the United States. Our graduate assistant, who was originally from South Korea, gave a presentation to explain the basic concepts of culture, to provide alternate viewpoints. I felt that "unpacking" the notion of culture was a start and would lead to more global, international concepts in the future. The teachers were questioned about the modern culture of today, and we talked about the culture of commercialism, global icons and marketing to children. As teachers responsible for the education of young children in a world where the alleged global culture is somewhat monolithic, their responses emphasized the importance of knowing one's family history and cultural background in the world today. Each team of teachers worked together to think of activities to incorporate the children's cultural backgrounds into their curriculum projects. Then they shared ideas with the group and learned from each other, so they were synthesizing new knowledge and collaboratively creating new curriculum activities for the children in their classrooms.

Teacher reactions to the staff development topic were varied, with many of them raising questions and wanting more direction about how to incorporate children's cultural backgrounds in their classrooms at different age levels. One of the teachers stated, "There is a lot more research I need to do to understand the cultural experiences in the class. I have to research more about geography and different cultures and then integrate that knowledge into projects." Another teacher said, "They need it to feel they fit in. They are the future. They must know about cultures. I was very glad that my eyes were opened to being broader in my projects. You must include cultures." The infant teacher said, "Culture has many aspects and it is different for everyone." A toddler teacher said, "I learned that children may be more excited to see parts of their culture in the classroom. I will make costumes and have children and families donate items." Reflecting on her own experience, a teacher shared that, "I learned that the culture from our countries are affecting how we live here in the United States." Teachers were starting to think about countries of origin, and how they might bring this into their daily lives with the children. It was not international thinking, but it was a good start, and I knew they would be experimenting with some of the concepts about culture we had addressed on that staff development day.

After much reading and researching on the topic of global citizenship for young children, I spent the summer formulating a professional development sequence of trainings that would move the Slattery staff into greater understanding and build self-confidence. I decided that we needed classroom observations and follow up dialogue sessions, too, so that the ideas presented in staff development days could be somehow brought into daily life in our classrooms. I had no idea if this would work or not, or how the children and teachers would respond. The director and I were both excited and uncertain at the same time, thinking that this was something new and important, but we had no certainty that we could make it happen. The plan at that point was to start integrating international ideas into the professional development days slowly, and for me to plan the research. I planned to collect data from the classroom observations and dialogue sessions, from children's individual artwork about the topic, and from parent surveys if we could get a substantial response. We had the challenge of "doing what was doable", which is never easy.

The change process was moving forward and, to my amazement, the university approved my concept and research. We were ready to proceed with the internationalization of our curriculum. The director's role was to support and further the teachers' learning processes on days when I wouldn't be there and to critically reflect with me about what worked and didn't work and to make suggestions for improvement. Our relationship was truly collaborative, and we both shared a global view of the world. We agreed to the change process that we believed had the best chance to work at Slattery.

Then we added one more crucial element that really jumpstarted the entire process. We decided that there would be a global committee at Slattery, consisting of teachers who had an international vision, were high-performing early childhood lead teachers, and who would be role models for the entire staff as the internationalization process unfolded. The plan was that they would meet with me and the director to review, create and continuously define and refine what we intended to achieve. A group of teachers, a graduate assistant who was a former teacher, the director, and myself, the faculty in residence comprised the global committee. We began meeting as a group initially during the planning year to solidify and begin our conversations and explorations; their perspectives were profound because members of the global committee represented Peru, Pakistan, South Korea, Israel, and the eastern and western regions of the United States.

Unfortunately we totally omitted any specific plan for evaluation, except the researcher's analysis of the anticipated data. I planned to spend a great deal of time at Slattery so that I could collect informal data, too, doing something like ethnography but not in a formal sense. Alternatively, we would be screening children for developmental milestones, as we always did, and we would keep our portfolios on individual children. Our project-based curriculum included visual documentation of the three phases of project based learning, and that would serve as a form of assessment as well. I recognized that evaluation and assessment at Slattery was crafted to focus on children's learning processes. We had not accounted for any assessments of internationalization of early childhood curriculum, probably because we were so focused on getting started.

Stage One: Planning Questions

Here are some questions to help you proceed during the planning year at your school:

1 Describe your school and the population you serve, including countries of origin and languages spoken.
2 What curriculum approach do you use for young children?
3 Is global content already embedded in the curriculum? If so, how is "global" defined?
4 What are your requirements regarding regulations, policies and accreditation?
5 How can you motivate your staff to build interest in internationalizing the curriculum for children? Is your staff already motivated and ready for change?
6 What is your school's location, and how does that impact on the curriculum?
7 What are the philosophical principles that represent your school's curriculum?

8 What is the vision of an internationalized early childhood curriculum that you want to achieve?

9 How does curriculum change happen in your school? Or, do you need to invent a change process that would work?

10 How will you initiate change to internationalize your curriculum? How can you plant the seeds of international thinking in the curriculum?

11 What are the elements of change in staff roles and responsibilities, the learning environment and in identifying resources?

12 Do you intend to provide professional development? How would you operationalize time allotment for professional development trainings?

13 What are the formal and informal methods you currently use to evaluate and assess your curriculum?

14 What new evaluation and assessment methods might you create to ensure that you are meeting your goals for curriculum change?

Stage Two: The First Year

The first year is a year of new beginnings in daily classroom practice, with all the anxiety, anticipation, exhilaration and frustration one can imagine and expect. Even with the most comprehensive planning process, and the most logical goal setting and distribution of responsibilities, it becomes quickly abundantly clear that people respond to new situations and to change differently, individually, based on their personalities, prior experiences with change and understanding of expectations and requirements. Some people are naturally comfortable and welcome change, while others resist change and require intensive supports and attention to move forward. In that context, your school will begin to internationalize early childhood curriculum.

Parents play a key role in internationalizing early childhood curriculum, particularly if they share whatever resources they have about different countries. Material resources such as books or food, or intangible resources such as storytelling or songs from other countries, can help young children gain an international perspective. Reinforcing children's learning at home can help the children to integrate their learning and transfer knowledge between school and home. Enlisting parental support is an essential step in the curriculum expansion process.

New ideas for internationalization and new ways to design classroom learning activities must be introduced to the teaching staff. Therefore, it is necessary to designate time for professional development, in whatever way is possible. Some schools fit in professional development during nap time, or lunch time, or they allocate staff development days every year for teachers to learn and grow. Professional development, at best, should be intentional and planned in a sequence of ideas for curriculum enhancement toward the goal of internationalization. If a sequential set of adult learning experiences is not possible, then the director should find innovative ways to share the information, according to what is appropriate in each school. Teachers can learn from new books, websites, blogs, online trainings and by inviting in guest speakers on the topic. Optimally, professional development topics should follow the interests of the teaching staff and extend their successes with children. Community resources and participation are beneficial and enriching as you internationalize the learning activities for children.

The director can lead the trainings or invite in someone with expertise in teacher training. Professional development can include an assortment of adult learning strategies and opportunities for acquiring new knowledge. Where staffing is minimal, or when children are living in regions of the world that are experiencing trauma and natural disasters, for example, full-day trainings may not be possible. Budget constraints may similarly limit the amount of time during the school day when teachers can focus only on their own learning. Directors generally find creative ways to share new knowledge with teachers, and that is a definite task to accomplish in Stage Two of the internationalization process. In addition, the director should continue to learn and develop, and time should be built in for the leadership to continuously learn about internationalizing curriculum, and about the world. Mentoring is a part of professional development, and the director is the obvious mentor to the teachers. Directors also benefit from mentors, who encourage them and give them concrete tools and skills to implement as the internationalization process unfolds. Confidence building is a critical component in the first year of this curriculum change process.

During Stage Two, the main emphasis is on work in the classrooms with young children, and the inevitable trial and error process of designing and implementing activities to help children understand that knowledge is global and we live in a big world, with many people living in different regions, with a variety of cultural backgrounds and experiences. Schools should build in a method for supporting teachers who are internationalizing their curriculum, and give them opportunities to share with each other and learn together. Teachers consider the children's developmental capacities in cognition and language, and their capacity to symbolically represent what they know through play, art activities, blocks, outdoor games, music, dance and in their conversations and explorations throughout the day. Indoor classroom environments may be altered to accommodate global trends and outdoor areas may be redesigned for global learning. Schoolwide international events and programs should enhance what happens in the classrooms, so that the children are included. A sense of pride for national identity and global citizenship should be part of a child's growing sense of self.

Teachers evaluate and assess their curriculums and the children's individual learning about the world through formal and informal methods. Success usually generates success in terms of internationalization. Much can be gained from activities that don't exactly work effectively because teachers can learn and do things differently the next time. When a teacher is busy figuring out how to internationalize the curriculum, an open mind and an attitude of learning is not only helpful, it creates valuable role modelling for the children. They are absorbing content knowledge, and essential dispositions and attitudes for lifelong learning about the world. Parents can give their feedback, too, and that is another form of informal assessment.

As you internationalize early childhood curriculum, a variety of resources and learning materials will be needed, depending on the ages of the children and their curriculum focus or themes. Young children learn through direct experiences of the world, through the five senses, and in the presence of loving adults and other children. They need learning materials that are age appropriate, safe and give them an equitable world view that is inclusive and highlights kindness for others. Whether you are locating, scrounging, purchasing and/ or making learning materials will depend on your budget and the needs at your particular school. In some instances, teachers attend workshops to learn how to create teacher-made materials for the children, like homemade books, lotto games, puzzles, maps and posters. In other circumstances, online resources and internet access may provide abundant international resources, for example, YouTube videos of animals around the world or music and dance from different countries.

Community resources can also be helpful if, for example, there is a local library, a children's theater or an art museum. Every community has its own international resources that can enrich curriculum. Community members are a great resource, and they can be invited into the classroom to share their stories, customs, hobbies and skills with the children. They can share cooking experiences, dance and make jewelry with the children, and many other creative learning activities that help children know more about the different regions and countries. People are the most valuable learning resource because the information is first-hand and honest, real primary information that can be shared through a caring approach to the children. Intergenerational learning can be extremely valuable, too, because young children enjoy the participation of grandparents, and if they come from a different country, children gain a larger view of the world. In year one, identifying and gathering international curriculum resources is continuous and involves teachers, parents and the director.

The Process at Slattery

Year two began with our annual parent meeting where parents are introduced to their children's teacher, the classrooms and the curriculum. There is a general feeling of excitement at the start of the school year, and in my role as faculty in residence, I give a little talk to the parents to highlight essential points in our curriculum and to give them a sense of confidence in our early childhood program. This year I spoke about our excitement about internationalizing our curriculum, aligning us with 21st century goals and giving children the skills and dispositions that they will need in the global economy and workplace, and an understanding of our interconnected world. I explained the methods for my research about global citizenship with children and invited them to sign consent forms to allow me to engage in classroom observations and to collect children's art from the four-year-olds at the end of the school year. The overwhelming majority of parents agreed to participate, with only four families not willing to give their consent. I explained that we believe that children can learn more if given the opportunity, and that creativity, collaboration and community would be our initial guiding principles. Slattery parents come from many different countries, and at the end of the meeting, some of them asked how they could contribute to the children's curriculum, and they wanted their children to learn to become global citizens. The parent response, fortunately, was unexpectedly positive and enthusiastic. They knew they would be welcome in the classrooms as well, and that teachers would collaborate with them to ensure successful learning experiences for the children.

Teachers at Slattery were introduced to the curriculum development and research project during the first two staff development days at the beginning of the year, before the children started school. We had hired new staff assistants, and they had no idea about project approach to curriculum, which is our major curriculum framework at Slattery. On the first day, I reviewed the components of project approach, and then we struggled together to imagine how we might internationalize classroom projects at the different age levels of the children. I reviewed the cognitive development of young children from three months to five years of age, spanning our population of children. Teachers were reminded about how children structure and organize their mental processes as their brains develop and as they engage in project-based learning. For new teachers, this was all new learning, and it really was a lot for them to absorb. Teachers worked together in their teaching teams and brainstormed about how we might internationalize project based learning, using the current classroom projects as examples. In a group process, the teachers helped each other learn. The infant and toddler rooms mentioned international music, sensory material from around the world, exposing children to different languages and exposing children to artifacts from different cultures, including dolls from other countries, dress up clothes, picture books and holiday celebrations. The teachers of three- and four-year-olds identified more conceptual learnings, such as people accessing water around the world, discussing family photos of families in their countries of origin, art activities and field trips, and inviting parents into the classroom who have particular expertise with culturally representative activities.

To further extend the teacher's learning, I asked them what they thought "international literacy" was and how they learned what they know about the world. Did they believe that what they saw on television and in the movies and social media was a truthful picture of the world? A complicated and provocative large group conversation followed about how stereotypes of people in other countries are shared and how we really form our world views. The teachers understood that not only are they responsible for their own global learning, but they should understand how young children develop their own international literacy and how teachers can transform children's world views and comprehension of differences among people. Basically, the teachers became more aware, and when I asked them how they would enhance their own international literacy, they enumerated a range of possibilities. These included reading books, watching movies and documentaries, travel, internet research, interviewing parents, keeping informed about world affairs and studying the globe. The teachers knew there was a great deal to learn. This was critical to enable our school to internationalize our curriculum, because teacher transformation would be central to the process. Truthfully, the teachers felt a little overwhelmed, but they were beginning to grapple with the new information, and a process of change had begun.

Day two of staff development introduced the research project into our work, based on the central research question, "What are the characteristics of global citizenship experienced and expressed by young children?" We thought of global citizenship as children's knowledge of the world and the interpersonal and social capacity to care for one another and to act compassionately as members of a larger community. I explained that this research would generate information that might contribute to the field of early childhood education, and suggest a direction for the curriculum of the future. The teachers had never participated in a research project, and I reviewed the elements and purposes of research, trying to demystify and simplify research methods.

The majority of teachers signed consent forms for me to conduct classroom observations and to document their teacher curriculum conferences. I shared with them the observation form I has designed and would use, and I answered their questions. I explained that in order to support the curriculum change process, I would be visiting classrooms in the mornings and engaging in dialogue sessions with the teaching team and the director during nap time when the children were asleep. My role was to help them identify goals, strengths and challenges, and to generally promote the internationalization process. They knew that there was no one correct way to do things, but rather a process of dialogue, and we would all be working together. Teachers understood that they were given the freedom to autonomously make changes and enrich their curriculum projects, and the director supported that approach. In our setting at Slattery, this research method for data collection was intentionally designed to undergird and support the internationalization process. We were fortunate to have a faculty in residence who could document the process for the purposes of research. But research is not necessary for internationalizing curriculum. Classroom observations and follow up dialogue sessions can be used in other schools, with the director or a teacher colleague conducting the observations. At the forefront of the curriculum change process was that Slattery teachers were reassured that they would be supported through the classroom work with the children and that we were working together.

The remainder of the second staff development day consisted of a presentation of the rationale for why we are internationalizing our early childhood curriculum and studying global citizenship for young children. We discussed the current state of curriculum, with commercialization, standards, evidence-based practice, assessment and data driven decision-making and the influx of technology. At Slattery, we follow a constructivist paradigm and actively create curriculum every day, following the interests of the children and building on their prior knowledge while encouraging them to ask questions and investigate. Investigation and a curriculum based on who the children are allowed us to internationalize with autonomy and our own sense of academic freedom. Our philosophy of professional development of the teachers corresponds to what we create with the children. Teachers were used to feeling empowered and autonomous in decision-making in the classroom. Self-reflection is encouraged, and dialogue is at the heart of the professional mentoring and learning. I consider staff development days as opportunities to explore ideas, to apply new knowledge and to introduce teachers to new possibilities for their teaching practice.

Teachers understood the multiple levels of identity development: local, national and global. Everyone felt strongly that we were teaching to promote democracy, no matter what a child's identity may be. Because we are situated in the United States, in an obviously Western cultural setting, democracy was and is highly valued. During staff development, we explored how we can teach for democracy and talked about how a project approach to curriculum is democratic. Teachers listed items such as freedom of choice and speech, equal rights in the classroom for all, equal opportunities to learn, freedom of information, voting rights, majority rule, respect for property and peaceful resolution of conflicts as optimal. They provided concrete examples of how they were teaching for democracy at the different age levels and emphasized the correlation between internationalization and democracy so that people can live together in the world.

The conclusion of day two pointed teachers in the direction of what was next in their classrooms when the children would return. They worked in classroom teams and brainstormed about internationalizing the learning activities and the classroom environment. For example, in the fours' classroom, they talked about how children were studying insects, and they planned to make a map of where insects live in the world and their habitats. The other four-year-old classroom stated that they had a parent come in and teach the children about the Indian festival called Diwali, and they were going to include other holiday celebrations in their project on light, along with a global exploration of solar panels and how they were used. The two-year-olds were planning to help the children learn about destinations through collecting souvenirs from different countries. They wanted to make costumes of regional cultural locations, to include in the dramatic play area. The babies' classroom teachers spoke about children's picture books and cultural food books, folk tales from other countries and country flags. The three-year-old classroom wanted to incorporate the art forms of different countries and mentioned Brazil and rock art, Guatemalan fabric weaving, Cuban landscape art, and English stone and metal sculptures. The other three-year-old classroom was studying insects, and they wanted to do habitats where ants live and make a bug and insect book that would correspond to a map of the world that indicated where the bugs live. The teachers enjoyed creative brainstorming, but were cautious about how they could actually translate these ideas into classroom activities.

After two days of immersion in international issues, I felt we were off to a good start, despite the anxiety because we had never done this previously. Teachers were a bit frustrated with me because I wouldn't give them a recipe of how to accomplish internationalization. I wanted them to learn by doing and gain strength by analyzing and improving on their teaching practice continuously. When new ideas are introduced, it takes time for teachers to intellectually "digest" and get ready to transfer their new knowledge into classroom practice. The process of internationalization in the classrooms had begun. The director described the teachers as "eager, excited and re-energized".

Classroom observations and follow up conversations continued throughout the year, and the graduate assistants also conducted classroom observations to document changes in the classroom environment and in activities. The purpose was to support and nurture the internationalization of curriculum and to make it clear that we were moving forward and that no one should feel isolated or lost. Having a process of support gave teachers confidence, as stated previously. It also focused the role of the director and myself, and teachers knew what the boundaries were and what kind of strong support would be provided. We wouldn't do it for them, but we would definitely be there for them to help when needed. Everyone knew that we were in the first year of a curriculum change process that would fundamentally change who we are as a school. A more detailed description of what happened in the classroom will be provided in Chapter 3 of this book, along with our "lessons learned".

Staff development days were scheduled through the year, and two very significant days were turning points in the staff's learning process. Topics for the trainings derived from my own research and my observations of what the teachers needed. There was no pre-set series of trainings, but rather subjects that emerged from what teachers were experiencing every day in their classrooms. As the year and the classroom projects progressed, I reflected on how rich and multifaceted the activities were and how creative the teachers had been. It became evident that they would learn best from each other at that point, and I decided that we would spend a full day moving from classroom to classroom so that teaching teams could present their projects and we would learn by seeing the classroom environment. When I presented this idea to the director, she suggested that teachers would benefit from an outline of questions for their presentations. That was great advice, so I created and distributed a brief description of global citizenship for young children, and then I added questions about how the process unfolded and how they internationalized the curriculum. I asked them to start their presentations with their own international backgrounds and experiences, so we would have a context for how they viewed internationalization. They had to report on the countries of origin in their classrooms, the languages spoken, travel experiences, and if the children had ever lived in different countries. They had to describe how the children express their understandings about the world. There were 16 questions about how the projects developed and how the teachers introduced the global perspective into the curriculum. I added self-reflective questions for the teachers about their own transformational learning processes.

This idea of presentations was really exciting for the teachers, and they enthusiastically, and sometimes nervously, shared their experiences and answered the questions as a teaching team in each room, and the other teachers were a receptive audience. At the end of each classroom presentation, the teachers had a question-and-answer session and reflected on what was presented, then I analyzed what we had learned about the internationalization process. We videotaped the classroom presentations, and this became a new and emergent data collection method that was not anticipated. Complex, deep questioning about curriculum was embedded in the presentations and the follow-up discussions. The depth of learning was formidable, and we were all happily surprised that the sharing of our curriculum projects yielded such rich information. This was indeed a substantive source of data. As a learning community, we witnessed how young children understand or don't understand the notion of global citizenship, and how this is developmental. I wondered if we were looking at a different phenomenon, and I was impressed by how much the teachers' lives had transformed by expanding the curriculum globally. There were unanswered questions and that "not knowing" increased our curiosity for further inquiry and exploration.

One major finding during Stage Two of internationalizing curriculum is that *knowledge is global and that children understand, experience and express this uniquely as individuals at different developmental levels.* The factors contributing to this were the skills of the teachers, the influence of families, and the children's levels of cognitive development and temperament. However, teachers and children were struggling with the concept of citizenship because it implied taking action to change the world. We all wondered if young children could do this, and if they were learning, instead, about the world in a meaningful way. It was challenging to articulate what we were observing, and so I decided to continue to observe it rather than labelling it prematurely.

Teachers continued to extend and internationalize their classroom curriculum projects for each age level of the children. My observations and discussions continued, as did more staff development days. The stories of the classroom will be described and analyzed in more detail in Chapter 3 of this book. I watched and listened carefully to all the changes taking place during

Stage Two: The First Year, and I began to collect my own notes to document, especially the informal conversations between parents and teachers, teachers and other teachers, and the director and teachers. Relationships were changing; I felt like I was an unofficial on-site ethnographer. It seemed as if people felt more comfortable talking about their countries of origin, what they might bring to the classroom and what international information children needed and could understand. There was more trust and more acceptance of the differences of others, and I believed that the interpersonal climate in the school was significantly shifting, in a positive direction. I began to notice disparities between how adults comprehend the world and how young children construct their own knowledge of the world based on what they are experiencing in school and the presence or absence of global perspectives in their homes.

The director was the key to the internationalization of Slattery's curriculum. She is an experienced, talented director who has the ability to effectively lead in an administrative capacity, managing day-to-day operations of the school and meeting all regulatory requirements and policy mandates. She is extremely supportive and wants the teachers to succeed with their own internationalization of the curriculum projects, and she illustrated this in her actions, conversations and even nonverbally in her body language and attitude. She communicates complete support for the teachers, children and families, and will go the extra mile to be helpful. I noticed that her ability to sustain confusion and disequilibrium was actually productive, leading to more complex solutions for the design of international learning activities. The director's flexibility, openness and creativity promoted positive change and gave the teachers a model for their own philosophical and intellectual inquiries.

Teachers were encouraged to learn from activities that didn't work out and to articulate what they learned so they could improve next time. The director was a mentor and at the same time she demonstrated and spoke about her own learning process, fostering a sense of Slattery as a learning community. I was a close collaborator with the director throughout the first year, especially, and felt fortunate that we could both openly discuss our mistakes in thinking and revise our planning processes based on observations of what was actually happening in the classrooms. Due to our extremely strong desire to be of service to humanity, we tried to do too much and our initial plans were a bit grandiose because we wanted to achieve too much, too fast. In Stage One: The First Year, we became very realistic and revised our expectations of the teachers, the children and ourselves. We recognized that we needed to spend time through trial and error, to integrate global thinking into the classrooms.

A major consideration was discovering and obtaining learning materials and resources for the classrooms, to enrich classroom projects and allow the children to directly experience global learning. We are a middle-class school located on a college campus, and we are fortunate to have internet access in the classrooms and some of the resources on the university campus, for example, a music room, a swimming pool, an outdoor meeting area and an oceanographic center. We are in a city named Boca Raton, which is suburban and typically contains community resources, for example, the mayor's office, the art museum, and a shopping mall. A large percentage of our parents and teachers were from foreign countries. They were eager to share their country's traditions, and they joined in classroom activities and brought in artifacts to share with the children. For example, a teacher in one classroom shared that in her country, people rode on elephants. They created (out of art materials) an elephant to ride on in their classroom, and it remains to this day in the dramatic play area. We did not spend a lot of money on resources because we scrounged around for items that would be a good fit with our curriculum, sometimes seeking out garage sales and consignment stores to find items that could be useful. Slattery teachers have had training in creating teacher-made materials, and their first impulse is to think about how they can invent learning materials rather than buy materials. They take initiative and help each other. For example, they created the different habitats of the world with children in recycled pizza boxes, which was just fine. South Florida is a tropical climate and objects from nature, like sea shells, palm fronds, and sand are used as learning materials in the classrooms, collected by teachers and children. The main expense, however, was children's books that were global in scope, matched the children's developmental levels, and related to the classroom projects they were investigating. The director supported the teachers by researching, locating and purchasing appropriate and useful children's books that would give the children a global point of view.

A global committee consisting of teachers, a graduate assistant, the director and myself met throughout year, usually on staff development days, to discuss, plan and review progress. Members of the committee were mostly from other countries who had become or were in the process of becoming United States citizens. They had an international perspective and almost all spoke two languages. In Stage Two: The First Year, they had responsibility for both internationalizing their classroom curriculums and participating on the global committee. In retrospect, I believe that this was an unrealistic demand because they were very focused on their own classroom processes. We began to extend our work together through dialogue about internationalization, and we all wanted to partner with schools in different countries. However, we were concerned about what collaboration is and how it would be received. The question of intercultural connection related to economic privilege became a central concern, and we explored our own privilege, living in a relatively stable economy while others in the world may experience poverty and food insecurity. Each member of the committee had a different world view, based on their own prior experiences.

The global committee worked with me to refine my initial research questions, and we tried to analyze the concept of global citizenship, each member contributing the perspective of their country of origin. I helped them understand the research process so they could explain it to other teachers when questions arose. For all the global committee members, this was their first encounter with research, and they understood that the research findings could substantiate what we intended to explore about children and internationalizing curriculum. We tried to define global citizenship for ourselves, and we discussed the meaning of citizenship as it affects human relationships. It was way too challenging to try to formulate a global network with schools in other countries when we were struggling to internationalize our own curriculum at Slattery. We chose to prioritize and focus on our own curriculum and what we were learning. Members of the global committee were deep thinkers and amazingly philosophical in their approach. They wanted to promote peace and to ensure that young children know they are part of a greater world. They asked questions about how people really learn from each other and how we might humbly and sincerely form relationships with people living in very different situations. We struggled to define our goals, and the goals kept changing. The global committee additionally attended an international conference on the subject of international education diplomacy together, and they interacted with colleagues from around the world. This was truly an enrichment experience for them, and it further complicated and developed their understandings. I believe that during Stage Two: The First Year, the global committee was really a "think tank" and forum for international communication and understanding, and throughout the process, they were internationalizing their daily life with children in the classrooms. At this point, members of the global committee became what I imagine to be "thought leaders" in our school. They were the intellectual anchors and thinkers, infusing their teaching colleagues with global knowledge and international ways of being in the world.

Professional development days were scheduled throughout the year, and I collaborated with the director to determine topics that would spark the teachers' interest and contribute to the curriculum change process we were engaged in. Year one of classroom change happened at a dizzying pace, with so much going on at the same time that it was often difficult to make decisions and be logical about next steps. Teachers continued to celebrate their successes, yet there were times when they felt discouraged and didn't know how to proceed. They often sought out the director for guidance and permission to take risks with activities. The director and I observed that the teachers benefitted from the professional development day classroom presentations, so we decided to give them another opportunity to do follow-up presentations on the next staff development day. I added in the subject of the creative arts because of the numerous ways that the arts can be international and participatory.

The next staff development day consisted of an activity for the teaching teams to reflect on their progress and respond to the following questions as a team:

1   How has your project transformed into a more globalized/ international project?
2   What have your children learned that contributes to their global competence and global citizenship?

3   What evidence do you have that children are learning and developing global competence and global citizenship?

4   How have you, as an adult learner, transformed as our curriculum has transformed?

The results of their responses revealed the differences in development, and how our youngest children were really growing in global competence; our four-year-olds were beginning to exhibit global citizenship because they were learning how to have an impact on the world. This realization would guide the continuation of our internationalization process and was another central finding of the research. The teachers also spoke openly about how this process had changed them, and they were becoming global citizens with an increasingly global perspective. I was amazed that in one year we could actually begin to understand the scope of how internationalizing our curriculum was actually changing our entire school. Our children were familiar with maps and began to understand what was actually represented on world maps. They knew there were other countries and other languages, and that daily life was going on in different places. In some classrooms, the children were talking about the "news" they watched on television, and in one of our classrooms, they made time for world news in their morning meeting. An international consciousness was emerging and evident.

Stage Two: The First Year: Questions to Guide Your Internationalization Process

Here are some questions to support your internationalization process:

1   How have you begun to incorporate internalization into your curriculum content?

2   How have you engaged parents to support children's growing global competence?

3   What is the director's role in supporting the internationalization of your early childhood curriculum?

4   What supports in your school and in your community are provided to promote internationalization?

5   What professional development content and sequence are you providing to support the teachers' success with curriculum, and with children and parents?

6   What ways are teachers encouraged to express their successes and challenges?

7   How are you building increasing global citizenship in teachers, and allowing their expression of successes and challenges, individually and collectively?

8   How have you documented the children's developing global competence?

9 What benchmarks have you set for the internationalization process in your particular cultural setting? How have you achieved your goals?

10 What continue to be the creative challenges in internationalizing your curriculum?

11 How and what have you learned from these challenges?

12 How are you planning for the second year of the internationalization process in your curriculum? What might you do differently next year?

13 Does your school's internationalization process reflect multiple viewpoints of the context of internationalization?

Stage Three: Consolidation Year

The second year of any curriculum change process naturally builds on the successes and challenges experienced during the previous year. If you actually set concrete goals for the first year, the beginning of the second year would be a good time to revisit those goals and identify new goals that have emerged and seem relevant. If you embedded research in the process, in the second consolidation year it is important to review research findings and plan accordingly. It is helpful to focus not only on the children, but on the teachers and their development and understanding. The director usually plays a key role in setting the goals and plans for professional development for the year ahead. Based on what was achieved in the previous year, new topics for professional development should be articulated and experiential ways to share this knowledge should be invented and planned in a sequence to build on prior learning and knowledge. In some instances, teachers may be consulted to identify topics of interest; however, they may not envision the big picture and goals, so their ideas should not be the only determining factor in the choice of professional development topics.

In the consolidation year, teachers feel more confident because they have experienced teaching successes with the children in the first year. They are generally more willing to take risks, and they have begun to develop international teaching resources such as children's books and dolls from around the world. Global teaching resources will vary from region to region in countries and in the world. Teachers have worked with parents on global understandings for their children, and there is a precedent set for a world view that is empowering and instructional. The context has already been established for everyone to be a learner, a global learner. The director's role will most likely shift in this second year because the teachers can be more independent. Allowing teachers to make increasingly important choices is one way that directors can be effective as curriculum leaders. Directors are responsible to ensure that any and all accreditation standards are met and integrated with the process of internationalization of the curriculum. Budgetary priorities are the responsibility of directors, frequently, in collaboration with an advisory board or owner, or school district supervisor. Adequate funding to support internationalization is absolutely necessary, and this is determined differently in each school.

During the consolidation year it is wise to provide opportunities for teachers to support each other across classrooms, in order for them to comprehend how children move through the school and different developmental levels of global competence and global citizenship. They need to serve as curriculum resources for one another, building a team spirit in the school to strengthen the curriculum internationalization process. Teachers can support each other in special and personal ways when they feel discouraged or frustrated, and they can share their successes with each other, too. School-wide events may be scheduled that promote the concept of internationalization. Teachers may be encouraged to reach out to early childhood colleagues in other countries to expand their perspectives and cultural contexts. In some instances, if financial resources are available, it would be beneficial for some teachers in the school to attend international early childhood conferences to gain a global view of the field of early childhood education.

Classroom and school environments play a role in educating children and families about the world. Environments speak loudly about what is valued and what learning takes place. To internationalize your school, the consolidation year provides an opportunity to take a look at what you may want to change about your school, in the classrooms and in the shared school communal spaces. For example, does the entrance to the school welcome children and families in different languages? What photos are displayed and what countries are represented, and what does the children's documentation or art reflect about global competence? Are there globes in the classrooms and/or maps of the world? Are the global images idealized or authentic, romanticized or real? Are there international children's books, newspapers from around the world and magazines that include a global perspective? How is technology used in the curriculum to give children an expanded worldview and real understanding? How do you share knowledge from parents or grandparents from other countries? How are international community resources shared? What else can you add to the environment to enhance the internationalization of curriculum? These are all considerations for individual classroom environments and for the school in general.

The consolidation year is a time to permanently or semi-permanently institutionalize the internationalization of your curriculum in ways that make sense and are developmentally appropriate. For example, you might want to include in your school calendar an annual international pot luck dinner for children and their parents, or create an international children's library of books for young children from around the world. The school may want to purchase memberships in international early childhood professional organizations, in order to include their publications and magazines in the teachers' resource room. You may want to purchase musical instruments from different countries so the children can experience playing music from around the world. Parents and/or teachers could put on an international fashion show for the children. There could be a yearly event where community elders who have lived in other countries come in and tell stories to the children, and these stories could be videotaped to form a global story archive for the school. The possibilities are endless, but once the changes are set and everyone knows what is expected every year, then the internationalization of the curriculum will be supported on an ongoing basis. This further strengthens children's learning and the transformational learning of parents and staff. No matter which curriculum your school uses, or who the populations consists of, or which languages are spoken, these kinds of international innovations can be achieved. Whatever changes are introduced would naturally have to be assessed annually to provide continuous improvement and to accommodate new directions in the classrooms and curriculum.

The Process at Slattery

Slattery engaged in multifaceted research on the topic of global citizenship for young children, and the teachers, parents and directors signed consent forms and the research was university-approved. Therefore it was imperative for me as the researcher to share my findings from the first year of the research. The teachers had actively participated in the research, including data from classroom observations, presentations, documentation boards, and artwork by the four-year-olds. Formal research and informal research methods emerged and provided a rich fund of data from which I could conduct an analysis. The research was qualitative and much of it was a hybrid ethnographic way of knowing because conversations in the hallways and other kinds of informal data was collected. I chose not to limit my data collection to the formal, preconceived formats initially intended. Instead, I was open to the emergent fund of data which reflected the authentic experience of what happened during the year. The findings were enlightening and informative, and helped us to plan for the year ahead. The overarching principle that emerged from the findings was that *knowledge is global*, especially now in the information age. Knowledge is shared across the world and is not situated in any one locale. What this means is that early childhood curriculum should reflect that reality; knowledge moves around the world and is a shared phenomenon. A brief summary of the findings are as follows:

- Professional development provoked new learning and investigation, and initiated a process of change.
- Transformational learning occurred for teachers, the director, and the researcher, as well as for the children.
- Children are passionate about making the world a better place, according to their own development and understanding.
- Transformation also happened for parents significantly for those who answered the surveys.

- The infant and toddler years provide the foundations for global competence.
- The development of global competence leads to global citizenship. Global competence means knowledge of the world, and global citizenship means that a person can do something actively to make positive changes.
- Global citizenship is essential for a democratic society in today's world.

Themes of meaning that emerged during the first year were:

- Young children's experience of community was expanded to include the local, state, national and international community. Community is a common theme in early childhood education, so this was a notable shift in understanding.
- There are many ways to understand the "world" and the notion of "international". Therefore, every person's understanding and experience should be valued and articulated. Collectively, we learn about the world from each other, so children should be given the opportunity to express their experience of the world and to hear each other. A person's understanding of the world is always expanding.
- The ability to adapt to change and to deal with change effectively is a skill that is learned through experience, starting with our youngest children. Change is directly related to increasing globalization and to the fact that changes will happen more rapidly in the future, and our children will have to adapt to change more quickly and effectively than ever before.
- Family relationships are transformed by children's growing awareness of global competence and global citizenship.

These findings were shared with the staff during staff development day at the beginning of the school year, so everyone was informed. The director and I had reviewed the findings and realized the significance of professional development in promoting and stimulating new thinking in teachers, leading to increasing global understandings. I also realized that the research process itself was an incentive and organizing structure. There were teachers who exhibited a range of global thinking and experience, and whose global citizenship identities were changing. We decided that professional development in the next year would continue to expand the teachers' global citizenship and identities, and I designated topics for professional development to further the teachers' learning processes. I also decided that, as part of the research, I would interview teachers in depth at the end of the year to gain insight into their growth as classroom teachers with an international perspective and their identities as global citizens. Their insights would be essential because teachers are the key players in this process, and their knowledge directly impacts young children becoming global citizens of the world. We recognized that we were fortunate to have a researcher on site, but considered that other schools may initiate research processes, too, by designating a teacher or "floater" or the director to gather data.

On the first staff development day, I introduced the topic of promoting global citizenship for young children through the creative arts. I brought in cloth art from Columbia, a South Korean doll and an elephant sculpture from Sri Lanka as examples. Creativity was an accepted paradigm at Slattery, and so I was building on the teachers' prior knowledge and experience. Philosophically, I believed that *the school is in the world and the world should be in the school.* Therefore, professional development activities included relevant visits to the community agencies and events that would give teachers an experiential understanding of this topic. A new art museum opened with several floors of exhibits representing different countries and cultures. The director and I visited in advance to see firsthand what the museum had to offer, and to arrange a meeting room space where we could debrief with the teachers. On the field trip, the teachers were asked to bring an iPad for each teaching team, to record specific artworks that would inspire them in their work with children.

On the day of the museum visit, teachers were excited and were given a brief presentation about international art experiences for young children, corresponding to the children's levels of visual symbolic expression. They learned about how to get inspired by art from different countries and to "creatively borrow" ideas from what adult artists create, and how to translate that inspiration into developmentally appropriate learning activities for young children. (They had experienced this approach previously, in past years, so "creative borrowing" was not a new concept to many of the teachers.) When we arrived, I initiated a "treasure hunt" in the art museum, and each teaching team was given an hour to locate five pieces of art that they could learn from and apply to their work with the children. I gave them written questions to follow, such as: 1) Where is the art object from and how was it made? 2) What are the artistic elements of the piece? (for example, portraits, decorative boxes, textures, free standing sculpture, collage, etc.) 3) How they might share this with their children? and 4) How could they use the art elements and invent age appropriate art experiences for the children? I also asked them what *they* learned from this art object. Each team had to take a photo of the objects on their iPad so they could later share their observations with the group at a debriefing. Our teachers were learning from the international group of artists represented at the museum.

After the "treasure hunt", we met to share our discoveries with each other. It was fascinating because some of the teachers were art lovers and visited museums regularly, and other teachers never before visited an art museum. There were a range of reactions among the group of teachers. It helped that they were given a clear task and focus for the start of the museum visit. The babies' class teachers identified the art letter wall with color contrasts that they saw at the museum. They thought they could recreate that back in their classrooms with the children's names and the hello greeting words in different languages. The two-year-old children's teaching team noted the sculpture of heads they had seen that used sand and dirt from all over the world. They thought that their children might do self-portraits with clay, and they could place the portraits on a world map. They mentioned that, as teachers, they were learning to synthesize information from around the world.

The teachers of the young three-year-olds identified an artwork titled *one alone again*, which included an abstract composition of lines and hidden images. They thought they could do this with the children and get them to discover hidden images in a larger artwork of lines. They also felt that the children would learn that lines have meaning, a definite pre-reading skill. The older threes' teaching team identified a collage of media events made of newspaper and cardboard. They thought their children could create a time-line collage of news and their own personal histories.

One of the four-year-old classroom teaching teams particularly liked a series of art photos of immigrants in boats, and they were inspired by the determination of the people represented in the photographs. They felt that the children could relate to the experience of really wanting something, and that they could additionally learn about placing photos in a sequence. They would try to get the children to take their own photos and see what they can develop. The same team identified the artwork of hats and flags of the world, which was relevant to their classroom project. They were interested in using this art form to help children understand how people can be united but different, and how countries can get along. They spoke about teaching the concepts of imports and exports and how countries connect. The other four-year-old classroom team liked the artwork made of flip flops and barbed wire, a free standing installation about the immigrant experience. They felt that their four-year-olds could learn about flip flops from other countries, and they could bring in a bilingual component, with the children making their own sea of flip flops and telling a story about it in two languages, English and Spanish. At the end of the conversation with the teaching teams, it was evident that profound learning had taken place, and that they were learning about different, international ways to see and experience the world, and that they were learning how to model the sharing of different perspectives in their classrooms. Flexible, diverse thinking is central for global understanding, and this professional development activity at the museum was therefore meaningful and transformative. Through direct experience, the teachers learned to connect their classrooms with the broader community, and they grew in their own global citizenship identities.

The second staff development day focused on intercultural communication, and how we understand and misunderstand one another across cultures. We thought together that if knowledge is global, it makes sense that relationships are global, too. Our school wanted to network and build bridges across the world with other schools for young children, an extremely ambitious endeavor, but we tried. Our population in South Florida consists of people from around the world, and the global network was initially in our own classrooms. Because we were involved in a curriculum change process, it became quite challenging to try to connect with the wider world directly. We tried to keep our attention on our curriculum as we internationalized children's learning activities, building global competence and global citizenship. During staff development, teachers participated in role plays that helped to bridge relationship building with different people in different lifestyles and culturally determined beliefs and values.

We explored how relationships are formed and what that means in different countries, with a group of teachers in our school from different regions of the world. They needed to hear each other describe the nuances and sensitivities necessary to promote intercultural communication. Then we reviewed the elements of cultural differences in communication, including what is taboo, how gestures are used, how mutual decisions are made, eye contact, proximity, the use of silence, overall body language, humor and what is considered funny, tone of voice and the impact of media images. The degree of media saturation in our environment was extensive because we are located in the United States and near Disney World. Access to technology and media is a determining factor in how children learn about the world and should be carefully examined as any school attempts to internationalize. The images that children see make a huge impression on their consciousness, and on their assumptions about the world. We explored the idea of teaching children to actively create media, like simple movies on iPads that express the reality they know, and not the reality that was manufactured and designed by someone else outside their cultural experience. Authentic cultural expressions can be shared. Our discussions revolved around how we communicate across cultures and what contributes to our success with relationship building. We concluded that the essential element was to build trust, and how that is communicated is variable. Teachers learned to avoid using slang expressions, to really listen to the other person, to find common interests and to slow down and speak clearly, paying close attention to body language. Relationships across cultures can be enriching and can extend a shared sense of global citizenship and basic human relationships in a context of peace.

In addition to staff development, we continued to convene a global committee of teachers who supported the internationalization of curriculum and contributed their expertise and insights into the ongoing process. We were striving to develop an international network, and meeting with frustration because we were trying to do too much. It was an overwhelming task to internationalize our own curriculum at the school, and we were trying to innovate in another area, and we just couldn't do it adequately. The responses we received from schools in other countries were somewhat confusing and we were not positioned to handle the degree of detail and attention required. The global committee was, however, very helpful in sustaining interest and collaboration in our school, and in identifying what they believed were key elements of internationalization. They stated that we could recognize internationalization by the evidence in the classrooms, and by international props and artifacts in the environment. They mentioned an enriched classroom with globally oriented learning materials, and the inclusion of the voices and international experiences of parents. We spoke about how everyone has a different conceptual schema of the world. The most significant issue that arose in the global committee was an appreciation for the conversations and play behavior of the children, and how their interactions and words reflected their growing global competence and citizenship. Children's play, the way they learn naturally, was a great aspect of curriculum to highlight, develop and examine.

The United Nations adopted its new Sustainable Development Goals (SDGs) while we were developing our new curriculum projects. Because 193 countries agreed to this and participated, we felt the support of the international community, and we absolutely felt that we were on the right track. In fact, early childhood education was included in the SDGs, acknowledging the value of our work and emphasizing the importance of the early years. It became apparent that the more we were open and aware about what was happening in the world, the more informed and energized our curriculum became. The teachers engaged in the curriculum with increasing levels of enthusiasm. We began to learn about early childhood education in other countries and we shared that information on a staff development day. The change in teacher's awareness of the world was beginning to really show in terms of the classroom projects. They approached their work with confidence and began thinking about the concepts internationally, and not only related to the local community. We discovered that books were helpful in exposing children to a global perspective. Some classrooms included YouTube videos of different places in the world. As a staff, we were energized and feeling increasingly competent.

The director and I identified the importance of children's thinking about global concepts and the internationalization of our curriculum. How young children conceptualize the world gives us clues about how to develop learning activities to foster and support their thinking. Recent discoveries in the field of neuroscience necessitated an emphasis on cognition and neuroscience in staff development, and it became obvious that we needed to understand the complexity of children's cognitive development related to their growing understanding of the world. In one of our professional development days, we explored children's cognitive development, how it interfaced with globalizing knowledge in the content areas and how children's conversations during the day showed us what they were thinking about the world.

We recognized that "the world" is a schema or mental construct that children understand differently in different countries of the world, and we wanted to learn about schools in other countries to learn more about this somewhat elusive concept of "the world, from the children's viewpoint. To that end, we decided to investigate early childhood education in other countries, and I gave the teachers a framework of questions and issues to research. We did not realize how ambitious we were. The teachers were fascinated with what they learned about early childhood education in different countries, but they did not necessarily connect what they learned with what the children were learning in their classrooms. At Slattery we have children from different countries, and the parents come to us with their own early childhood experiences from their own childhoods. Nevertheless, we were unable to move forward with any significant activity in terms of networking, and although we persistently tried, we continued to confront obstacles in communication and expectations. We were oriented toward dialogue, and we quickly learned that not all teachers around the world think the way we do. As a school, we had to look in the mirror, too, and recognize that we frequently try to take on too much and sometimes frustrate ourselves, resulting in burnout. From a research perspective, I identified this as a "culture of busyness" in our school, with multiple goals overlapping and demanding our time and attention.

One of the hallmarks of successful, planned curriculum change processes is the maintenance of a stable staff, so that ideas do not have to be retaught and reintroduced, and everyone can basically be moving forward together. In reality, however, that is not always the case. We experienced the unexpected departure of a lead teacher and, following that, I needed to take a temporary leave of absence for personal reasons. Some of our classroom assistants also either left or were relocated in different classrooms. Staff changes required the director to take a more instructional role in curriculum, to redistribute some tasks in the school, and to hire a new lead teacher. The role of leadership shifted, and an effort was definitely made to stabilize the staff, and that was actually accomplished. The staff and the director grew in their resilience and ability to adapt to circumstances and to stay on task with the goal of internationalization.

Stage Three: Consolidation Year: Questions to Guide Your Internationalization Process

Here are some questions to guide your process during the consolidation year:

1 What goals have you met, and how were you successful in internationalizing your curriculum in the first year?
2 How have you changed or refined your goals?
3 How have teachers' understandings of internationalization been reflected in their classroom curriculums?
4 How are the teachers increasing their experience and identities as global citizens?
5 What planned and unanticipated staff changes have occurred, and how have you ensured stabilization of the staff?
6 How are teachers sharing their knowledge and success with other teachers, to build a school culture of internationalization?

7   What classroom instructional strategies, from a developmental perspective, have contributed to the children's growing sense of themselves as globally competent, leading to their identities as global citizens?

8   How have parents and other family and community members been successfully included in curriculum enrichment to achieve global perspectives?

9   What international resources continue to be helpful within the school and within the community?

10   What topics for professional development are you providing now and in the future to promote the internationalization of curriculum?

11   What ways have you utilized technology (if it is available) to promote children's learning about the world?

12   How has the director's role shifted, and what are the new leadership priorities?

13   What budgetary and resource allocations have changed to support the internationalization process?

14   What schoolwide changes have you implemented in your event calendar?

15   What schoolwide changes have you implemented in the physical environment of the school and the classrooms?

16   What unanticipated situations have you encountered as a school, and how have you built school resilience, resulting in the strengthening of the internationalizing of your curriculum?

17   What obstacles, challenges and dilemmas remain and how will your school recreate these issues and reframe them into opportunities to promote the internationalization of your curriculum?

18   How are you sharing what you are learning with the early childhood professional community around the world?

Stage Four: Independence and Integration

Stage Four is actually the third year of classroom implementation and schoolwide change, and the process of internationalization of the curriculum is generally part of everyday classroom practice and the culture of the school. Teachers do not need intense professional development, and they are able to function independently because global competence and global citizenship have become integrated into an internationalized early childhood curriculum, corresponding to the developmental levels of the children. The director does not have to focus specifically on this dimension of the curriculum and can attend to other dimensions of the school's functioning. By this stage, the school's website and promotional materials have probably been adjusted to reflect the international perspective, and parents are informed about this when they enroll their children. Processes are in place to help teachers locate the resources they need to enhance and globalize their curriculums in the classrooms. In many schools around the world, accreditation and evaluation is required, and schools need to determine how internationalization fits into their respective accreditation systems.

In this stage, it is still helpful to continue enthusiasm for learning, maintain expectations and provide support on an ongoing basis. Some examples might be providing monthly teacher's meetings to discuss and ensure the continuation of global perspectives in the curriculum, possibly forming a global committee of teachers to help the school connect with other schools around the world, perhaps initiating an action research project or more formal research project to document and share global perspectives, and finding a venue for teachers to continue to develop their own global citizenship and their connection to the early childhood profession around the world. Without these kinds of supports, the curriculum will not necessarily continue with the passion for internationalization, and some teachers may tend to lose interest in further developing knowledge about internationalization.

The Process at Slattery

Slattery did not have the benefit of the researcher consistently during this stage, and they proceeded independently, with some strong successes and some areas that need further attention. It was a challenge for them to integrate all they had learned and accomplished. Observational data and summaries of the classroom curriculums, part of the research, were collected. These observations demonstrate that most teachers continued to co-create internationalized curriculum projects with the children. However, without the researcher present, a few of the teachers lost their focus and did not specifically include the global dimensions of children's learning. That was disappointing, and it reflects the lack of structural support for continuing the internationalization process. We never anticipated that such a support system would be helpful. Most teachers did, however, enthusiastically continue to globalize learning for the children and were happy to do so. We learned that a support structure would have been optimal, and started to think about how this could be accomplished in the future.

An outstanding success during this stage came through the inspiration of the director. She was free to focus on the whole school, and she decided to develop a large, multi-site children's garden with the input of the teachers in each classroom. The garden spaces included a butterfly garden at the entrance to the building, individual vegetable garden beds for each classroom, and a huge garden on the land behind the school building. The unusual feature of this large garden is that there are sections for plants from around the world, representing many of the countries of origin of the children and families who attend the school. The garden is a work in progress, and it is definitely unique because it will expose children to plants from different countries of the world, building a global sense of environmental appreciation, and following one of the most prominent United Nations Sustainable Development Goals. We look forward to opening day of the garden, and all the experiential, hands on learning that the children will experience.

I had shared my findings with the staff, especially the "big picture" ideas that had emerged, and this was encouraging and intriguing for the teachers. Respecting the fact that Slattery teachers are extremely busy, we are struggling to find time and energy to begin and try to complete any form of further research. Our conversations have centered on different areas of interest for each lead teacher, and we want to honor their interests and encourage them to explore topics that are relevant to them. All teachers were interested in publication as a way of sharing their learning with teachers around the world. However, thus far, those discussions have not resulted in any concrete actions.

Stage Four: Independence and Integration: Questions to Guide Your Internationalization Process

Here are some questions to stimulate your thinking and curriculum process during the fourth year of independence and integration:

1   What support structure(s) might you create for the teachers to maintain enthusiasm for continuing the internationalization of your curriculum?
2   How is your accreditation and evaluation process impacted by the internationalization of your curriculum? How can your school benefit from this?
3   How might you design and implement innovative schoolwide projects and/ or research related to the internationalization of your early childhood curriculum?

Summary

This chapter has provided guidelines to stimulate, challenge and encourage you to embark on the journey toward internationalization of your early childhood curriculum. Today our schools are in the world, and the world should be in our schools, according to the developmental levels of the children and the growing identities of the teachers as global citizens.

An overview of each stage has been provided, followed by a description of our process at Slattery as an example, and questions to serve as guidelines for the internationalization of early childhood curriculum in any location in the world. Four stages have been identified:

- Stage One: Planning
- Stage Two: The First Year
- Stage Three: Consolidation Year
- Stage Four: Independence and Integration

Changing a curriculum is never totally predictable, and unexpected circumstances occur along the way, often leading to better outcomes than were initially planned. Flexibility is the key, and patience and respect for the work of our teachers and directors. At every stage, imagination and discovery is required, along with critical observation of the children and self-reflection by the teachers and the director. During the planning process, make sure to include what you know you can accomplish, along with other items which may be difficult. That way, you build success upon success, and you will not be easily discouraged. It is a slow process, well worth the effort when you observe children playing and including global thinking naturally in their everyday conversations and play themes.

The next chapter gives you a glimpse into the daily curriculum projects at Slattery, and what we learned that may be valuable for your school, as suggestions. In an increasingly interdependent world, we are always exploring what is possible, and pushing the limits of what young children can learn about the world.

3   Stories from the Classrooms

Introduction

We didn't start our work with a theoretical or intellectual structure because we had the audacity to believe and hope that internationalizing our early childhood curriculum, and exploring global competence and global citizenship with young children, was forging new curriculum "territory". And indeed it was. Most of the time, the children's learning experiences and reactions guided us and caused us to reflect on our own perceptions and expectations of internationalization. We were aware that, in early childhood education, there has been a history of including the world in the classroom, derived from the progressive theories of John Dewey and the ground-breaking ideas of Maria Montessori. As previously mentioned, global citizenship and global education were terms that were buzzwords that seemed to demand everyone's attention. We wanted to discover what was real for us, in our school, with a particular group of children and families and teachers. Cognizant of the differences in development for all children, we followed developmental appropriateness as it applied to our children and families. Harriet Cuffaro (1995, p.103) states in her discussion of developmental appropriateness, "It is a phrase that evokes mixed feeling: my willingness to give attention to development and my resistance to the judgement implicit in the word *appropriate*. Whose view of development? Who decides?" Teachers at Slattery began questioning and reconsidering what children showed us they could actually do, and we stubbornly refused to allow our preconceived expectations to place limits on the children. We recognized that our discomfort might provoke and promote innovation and definitely more inquiry, and that could be uncomfortable. Arthur Costa and Bella Kallick express it beautifully in the following quote: "Our students are *in* the 21st century, and they are waiting for the teachers and the curriculum to catch up" (Costa and Kallick in Jacobs, 2010, p.211).

The field of multicultural early childhood education, with its research, theories and practice, has expanded and supported the values and parameters for young children growing up with an appreciation of human differences, and the nonjudgmental ability to form friendships across cultures. Numerous pioneers, such as Leslie Williams, Louise Derman-Sparks and

Patricia Ramsey, have lead the way and opened our eyes to a range of differences among people and how we think and react to cultural differences in our classrooms. Ramsey raises the concern that teachers risk oversimplifying complex issues for children, in an attempt to make ideas clear and meaningful, and that we must help young children live with contradictions and yet maintain their optimism in an imperfect world (Ramsey, 2015, p.21). It is imperative to deconstruct stereotypes and to avoid oversimplified definitions of culture based on single experiences and/ or cultural artifacts. In the age of social media and technological changes rapidly providing us with new communication platforms, children are faced with an enormous amount of information about other people, about the world, and about how to negotiate and actively participate in society and the world, as they comprehend these concepts. Young children construct their worlds from the information they receive and the interactions they experience. James Banks identified multicultural education and its goals, while other leading multicultural educators urged us to explore different contexts for learning, and the troubling issues of racism, discrimination and privilege, daily realities that young children as exposed to, in person in schools and communities, or indirectly through a variety of media-related communication venues. In early childhood curriculums in our classrooms, there is a difference between the multicultural learning materials we provide, and the multicultural factors which impact on the complex webs of relationships among children, teachers, parents, and directors. We are reminded by Janet Gonzalez-Mena that "the differences in perspective and worldview can show up in communication styles" (2008, p.34). Multicultural education is desirable for young children, and multicultural learning materials such as multicultural dolls, music, games and books are frequently included in classroom learning environments.

Slattery is not a bilingual program; however, we do our own unique method of Spanish integration into the children's classroom projects, following their interests. Every week, a special teacher comes into each classroom and does a Spanish lesson with the children on the topic of their chosen projects, so the children are interested and invested in learning. Because we have multiple languages represented at Slattery, and because many of the teachers speak a second language, the parents voted and selected Spanish. This reflects our surrounding community in South Florida. Starting with the babies and through each age level classroom, we expose the children to Spanish as a significant part of our internationalized curriculum. Children need to understand that people around the world speak in different languages, and even if they are not necessarily fluent in a second language, they learn that communication can be different among different people. We believe that this exposure broadens their perspective of the world and their place it the world community.

Multicultural early childhood education provided the foundation for our internationalization process at Slattery. We had been assessed and had received high scores in multicultural curriculum in our previous accreditation experience, so we felt confident in encouraging children's appreciation of differences. We had been cautioned not to present a tourist approach, with superficial learning for the children. However, we recognized that the world had changed and that there were several interconnected aspects of society that all lead to the idea of global competence and global citizenship, described in Chapter 1 in this book. I was quite surprised when someone asked me why little children should be bothered by knowing the world. The majority of the teachers embraced the idea of internationalization, and yet there were some who agreed because they wanted to please the director and the researcher. There were one or two teachers who quietly complained and didn't understand why we were doing this, no matter how many times it was explained to them. Teachers were responsible for integrating the state learning standards, conducting parent meetings, and co-creating curriculum with the children. Although it appeared initially overwhelming, after continuing professional development days filled with international ideas and adult learning activities, they were ready to basically get started and globalize their classroom curriculums with the children.

Research methods to gather data in the six classrooms consisted of an observational tool that targeted specific areas of the learning environment and the interpersonal dimension of relationships, through children's play and conversations. Observations were conducted at Slattery in all six classrooms over a two-year period. In year three, classroom data was collected through observations and dialogue with the teachers about their projects. Additionally, informal, emergent methods, such as teachers reporting on their projects during staff development days and reflective conversations with teachers, the director and the researcher, provided insights into how curriculum decisions were being made in our early childhood setting. Data analysis didn't follow the formal rules of research because we had to revise and change what we were doing as we proceeded. We began by focusing on global citizenship, and then after a year we realized that we were looking at the foundations of global competence and global citizenship, and that it followed the children's development over the years. The one basic dimension of global competence that did emerge, however, was *equipping children to accept and embrace change in positive and productive ways*. The data also indicated that the topics for our curriculum projects in each classroom tended to *correlate with the United Nations Sustainable Development Goals, without specifically consciously intending to so*. It became clear to the researcher that *the teachers were essential in the curriculum internationalization process*. We were examining the way children understood the immediate, local communities they live in, and the wider world as they could conceive of it. This meant that *we were always moving from local to global in our curriculum*. And we were fascinated and energized by the fact that *young children could learn more about the world than we anticipated*, and it was important to follow their lead and their investigations; we didn't want to limit what they could understand.

Infant and Toddler Classrooms

Teachers in the infant classroom really struggled with what this meant for their children and with how babies could begin to be part of a school that was "going global". At first the teachers made a map of the world with names of the children and yarn lines connecting with each child's family's country of origin. When I came into the room as the researcher, to observe, there was a revealing moment that demonstrated that the teachers wanted to participate but didn't know how to scale the concepts to the children's developmental levels. Infants are experiencing their first separation from their parents and, therefore, attachment with new and significant adults, the teachers, is a major developmental goal. The children are in the sensory-motor stage of development, and their brains are growing rapidly as they explore the environment around them. They touch, taste, smell, hear and see the world, and they learn from direct experience and immersion in sensory activities. Infants are in motion, feeling their bodies in space and learning to crawl and walk at their own pace, in their own time. Babies learn what language is and that sounds and words are a way to interact with other people. Conversational exchanges of single utterances and gestures begin to occur, and infants watch the world and move through it randomly at first and then intentionally, with a desired purpose. They learn that language is used for communication, and they are in the initial stages of imitating word sounds and playing with sound production. Trial and error learning and repetition characterize their play behaviors, and they are often solitary yet aware of what's happening around them. Given these developmental characteristics, how did our teachers approach the idea of internationalization? What learning experiences could we provide to give them a foundation for global understanding?

In the first year, the teachers identified their project as *animals* because the children were fascinated with all kinds of animals. The classroom had multicultural dolls and pictures of food from around the world. The children began to demonstrate kindness by occasionally helping each other, and even patting each other on the back as acts of caring, especially when a friend fell down and possibly started crying. At circle time, the teachers introduced a picture of a Chinese water dragon, but the children didn't really understand that it was related to another country because their experience was in the here and now. The year progressed, and the children became aware of one another and became attached to their teachers. They would run to the fence at outdoor play time, and they seemed curious as they noticed the world around them. The teachers were challenged to think about internationalizing a curriculum for babies, and they decided to start with the animals in the children's lives. The learning activities included providing a variety of stuffed animals, books about animals, and bringing in real animals who were pets, such as a cat, a Siberian husky dog and a Maltese dog. They sang animal songs and took the children outdoors to find and name animals. The children discovered iguanas, spiders and ducks, sometimes just by pointing at the animals in delight. A petting zoo visited our school and the children got to touch, hear and smell different animals, and they were thrilled. Teachers researched the origins of some of the animals and decided to introduce animals by art projects that the children could experience directly. They learned about a different animal every week. For example, they made painted turtles, they made owl feet, and they made raccoon tails. Teachers introduced some exotic animals, too, but it was difficult to see how much the children really understood. A map titled "A World Outside of Their World" was created by the teachers and shared with the children, beginning to expose them to the idea of visual maps where something represents something else. The children discovered and pointed to animals on their printed tee shirts and were able to name them, but they didn't have a concept of the world beyond their immediate experience.

The foundational skills for global competence were definitely being developed because a sense of self and bonding to significant adults is essential before being able to relate to other people. Children's curiosity was peaked though intensive investigations about animals, enabling their neurological development to steadily increase and extend structurally. They were beginning to understand that there are other people in their world, which is similarly foundational for global competence. By providing new hands on experiences, the children began to invent their own simple cognitive theories about how the world works, and they saw themselves as competent to take action, move around and explore. These are dispositions and habits that would serve them well as they continued to grow in global competence. The teachers learned on an adult level. Also, the parents got excited about the idea of global competence, and so the adults transformed their perspectives in the first year and began to see the world differently, in a larger sense. The openness to new learning was celebrated and is a hallmark of continuing learning, critical to the development of global competence.

The next year, the babies' room selected *things that move* as their classroom project. During this year there was a change of lead teachers in the classroom, and the new teacher was very creative. Many sensorial arts activities were provided for the children. They studied vehicles and made painted truck wheel paintings, circular sponge wheels for a bus, scribble drawings of roads, a traffic light with colored paint prints and a small collage on canvas of drawn train cars. What was significant and different this year was that the teachers embedded global learning into the children's activities, talking with them about different countries while they were making colored prints of traffic lights and showing them photos of busses, trucks, and street signs from around the world in circle time.

The teachers had shifted their own understandings, and they were able to share this with the children. It is questionable, though, how much babies from six months to a year can conceptualize about a world beyond their everyday reality. However, the teachers provided innovative and interesting learning experiences that extended children's learning, giving them the experience that there is always more to learn, which is foundational for global competence. The teachers felt more confident in what they were doing and did not look for immediate feedback from the children, recognizing that they were building a foundation for future global competence and global citizenship. This awareness permeated the babies' classroom. During a brainstorming session, the teachers stated that they felt that it was very important to expose the children to the world outside their own environment because the children would be advanced developmentally in comparison to those who were not exposed to a global curriculum. They felt that they were becoming globally competent and hoped to contribute to peace in a few generations. The teachers reported that they thought that teaching empathy was essential for global understanding, since babies are naturally egocentric and are beginning to shift to awareness of the feelings of others. They enjoyed their conversations with the parents about their different cultural backgrounds, and felt that they were learning and growing as global citizens. The teachers were learning about the world, and their openness to new experiences similarly increased.

The two-year-olds' classroom at Slattery is an exciting and nurturing educational environment, where the children are encouraged to actively explore their classroom and adjoining outdoor playground and to develop relationships with their teachers and with each other. They are learning about themselves, what their bodies can do, and that there are other children who have needs and feelings just like they do. Two-year-olds are in motion like the infants, and they are gaining control of their physical bodies with a particular emphasis on potty training. They are learning through their senses, and they are becoming aware of the beginnings of visual symbolic representation. That means that they are scribbling, randomly at first and then more purposefully, and they are recognizing that visual images have meaning, although they assign changing meanings to their scribbles and little by little their visual images become a bit more stable and actual visual schema begin to form. They are learning that words are powerful and can be effective in getting their needs met, instead of grabbing and hitting others. Language is definitely connected to relationships and activities in their growing minds, and they experiment with language by playing, singing, and trying out simple conversations.

In the midst of all this intense and multifaceted development in the twos' classroom at Slattery, the teachers were totally at a loss to begin to internationalize the project-based curriculum. They just didn't know where and how to approach the introduction of global competence for two-year-olds in the sensory-motor stage of development, who are engaged in the sensory world of here and now, and who are beginning to make sense of it through words and visual symbols, and relationships. They appropriately identified a project on *food,* a subject that usually holds the attention of almost every two-year-old. The project included documentation boards, children's authentic art activities, language experience charts, and many child-centered learning activities. The classroom was positive and joyful, and children had choices of activities such as drawing and printmaking, using Play-Doh to make pretend fruit, feeding doll babies with toy milk bottles, listening to stories about food, and eating together at lunchtime while talking about their different foods. Outdoors they enjoyed running and climbing, playing with balls, riding small tricycles, and observing the natural elements around them, like birds, trees, salamanders and clouds. They pretended to be making food and serving each other and the teachers. There was great teamwork among the teachers, and the children had formed secure and trusting relationships with the teachers. All this was wonderful and a rich, high-quality learning experience for the *food* project, but it wasn't global in any way, and the teachers were perplexed. They needed support and feed-back from me as the researcher and from the director.

We arranged a post-observation dialogue and talked about the whole idea of internationalizing curriculum for two-year-olds. To begin with, we dis-covered that there were children in the class whose families spoke Spanish, Turkish, Armenian, French and Russian, as well as English. It became evident that the children knew that there are other countries because their parents or grandparents were talking about this and sharing their cultures at home. How could we bring this knowledge into our classroom of two-year-olds? How could we interact with the parents and be more welcoming than we had already been? We brainstormed about cooking activities in the classroom, with foods from different countries, and inviting the parents in to share their special family recipes. This idea initially seemed somewhat new and overwhelming. We also realized that the children seemed to love books and that perhaps we could read them books about foods from other countries and make books about their cooking experiences. These all seemed like valuable activity ideas, but because this was the beginning of globalizing the curriculum, they were not really implemented at this point. The teachers were doubting that two-year-olds could gain a global perspective at all. They did, however, strongly believe in educating children to embrace diversity and to be kind to all people all the time. Importantly, the teachers realized that they had a lot to learn about the countries of origin of the children, and they began to think about their own countries of origin and how that influenced who they are today.

The teaching team identified the specific social-emotional skills that form the basis of global competence for two-year-old children. These skills are: encour-agement and support for new adventures, respect and understanding of another person's feelings, the awareness that we all impact on other people emotion-ally, self-awareness, trust that the adults and other people are good and posi-tive, and exposure to and experience with different cultural experiences. They wanted the children to learn to be loving and kind to everyone, and to under-stand that they are Americans and citizens of the world at the same time. They acknowledged that this may be somewhat cognitively advanced for the chil-dren, nevertheless, by exposing them to different people, languages and experiences, they felt that we were promoting global competence which would eventually lead to the children's global citizenship. Helping children to master the phenomenon of change and transitions was recognized as essential for global competence, too, because the world keeps changing every day.

The next project in the twos' classroom was the unusual subject of *bees*. The children were totally focused on bees while they were planting outdoors in their garden, and they wanted to explore and learn more and more, to everyone's amazement. The children's energy and enthusiasm was contagious, and the teachers got excited about the bees, too. Because the children's language is limited at this age, the teachers had to watch them carefully to figure out what actually caught their attention with the bees. They began the project by creating a tree and beehive with paper towel rolls, and made three dimensional bees with clay. This was followed with a virtual learning experience where they viewed the behavior of bees in a video. A parent who was a beekeeper came into the classroom and brought honeycombs for the children to see. This led to an exploration of honey, with children tasting and feeling and smelling different types of honey. Parents went to the library to find bee books for the children. The children made bee costumes and pretended to be bees in dramatic play, acting out the roles of different bees. They even made a table cloth about bees that they used at lunchtime.

And then something remarkable and extraordinary happened. The teachers put up a world map and placed bee pictures on countries that represented the children's families' countries of origin. There were pictures of bees on the world map, with the name of the bee and where it's found. For examples, they showed North American bees for children from the United States and Canada. The children watched a video on Maya the Bee, in Spanish, and the teacher worked with them to identify and compare their body parts with those of the bees, in Spanish and English. On a two-year-old level, they were doing bilingual comparative anatomy of people and bees. The children learned that there are bees all over the world, and that bees have bodies like they do. *A profound shift had taken place in the two-year-old classroom curriculum. Knowledge became global, and that is absolutely foundational for the development of children's global competence.* The teachers demonstrated that they, too, understood that knowledge of subject content extends throughout the world, and that it is the teacher's role to bring that global knowledge into the classrooms of young children today.

The next project in the two-year-old's classroom was strengthened by teacher confidence, based on the previous bee project's success. Teachers noticed that the children were playing in dramatic play with fire trucks, firefighter costumes and fire trucks, in a very enthusiastic way, over a longer period of time than usual. The subject of the *fire station* became the next curriculum project. They invited in a teacher who was in school learning to become a firefighter, and he arrived in the classroom wearing firefighting gear and a hat and gloves. The children got to try on his gloves and talk with a real fireman. They learned about firemen protecting citizens and preventing "boo-boos". After that experience, the children made their own firefighter costumes in the classroom and played with them in dramatic play. The Spanish teacher taught them about firemen in Spanish, reading a bilingual book on the subject called *Fire! Fuego!* By learning about their project in a different language, they were in fact learning that people speak differently about the same kinds of ideas, another skill that undergirds global competence. The children were transferring knowledge and beginning to make cognitive connections. Later in this project, the local fire department came to visit and read a book to the children, emphasizing that they should not be scared. The teacher emphasized that through teamwork we all work together to make sure everyone is safe, once again demonstrating the value that we are responsible for one another. The children created their own fire truck out of cardboard boxes that were painted, with chairs inside so they could play. The classroom environment was filled with local knowledge about what a *fire station* is and how firefighters can keep people safe and that we all work together.

The documentation board for this project then went to the next step and included a chart of fire trucks around the world, with the words for "fire trucks" in different languages. The parents helped supply the words, and the teachers appreciated their contributions. Once again, they taught the children that knowledge is global, that there is a world beyond their world and they are part of it. We are all interconnected and, indeed, knowledge is local and global, and all nuances in between. The teachers noted that they are exposing children to communities all over the world. In their words, the teachers stated that they "do global awareness to open the door for global citizenship". They found out that what they previously believed wasn't possible was actually doable and successful, and it resulted in children learning and developing their minds. They additionally learned that they are global citizens and that their experience and understanding of the world is increasing as they teach from an international perspective.

The Younger Three-Year-Old Classroom

The younger three-year-olds' classroom was composed of children from different parts of the world, so the population was international to begin with. The children's families spoke six different languages at home, including Thai, Spanish, Hindi, Turkish, Mandarin Chinese and Romanian. The teachers came from different countries as well, and the lead teacher was an active member of Slattery's global committee. Internationalization should have been easier for this class in the beginning, but it wasn't. They were challenged by the internationalization curriculum process in many of the same ways that the other teachers experienced. Three-year-old children are learning about themselves and about how to interact and play with others. They are learning vocabulary rapidly and experimenting with cause-and-effect thinking and trying to formulate and understand interrelationships, similarities and differences, time sequences, and categorization. They are learning to use language for communication with others to negotiate ideas and play, to increase their attention spans and to delay gratification somewhat, all skills that will eventually lead to appropriate executive functioning. We were encouraging creativity and problem-solving skill development, too. In addition to the intensive and complex developmental growth the children were experiencing, we had a number of children with special needs in this class. For example, we had a child on the autism spectrum, a child with sensory integration issues, and a child with low tone and attentional problems. That further complicated the curriculum internationalization, and it wasn't something we had planned for or anticipated when we began to integrate a global perspective into the classroom. It became important to not only incorporate an international content in our curriculum, but we are an inclusion program, so we needed to adapt our global curriculum activities for children with special needs.

The initial project was *food*, something almost every three-year-old is extremely interested in. The teachers were from different cultural backgrounds, and they were excited about sharing the foods from their countries. A Haitian teacher made plantains with them, and the teacher from Thailand introduced pad Thai. Building on children's sense of learning about living in communities, the teachers felt that the topic of community was central to what young children need to comprehend, and they were committed to helping children learn respect for others. They began with the community around the children first, and then expanded to introduce children to the idea of a globe and map of the world. Videos of other countries were shown to the children and discussed with them, starting with their reactions and expanding whatever ideas the children brought forth. The food project proceeded with the expected high quality activities and materials related to food, like posters of fruits and vegetables, children cutting fruit with plastic utensils and eating fruit salad, singing a fruit salad song, sorting seeds and exploring dirt, and learning where food comes form. They planted bean seeds and sunflower seeds, with pots for each child, learning about protein and reading books about food. One of the mothers from Turkey came in and made Turkish soup with the children. The children talked about food many times a day, especially when someone had a birthday and they had birthday cake, a frequently universal experience. They talked about food and a range of other things, like Disney World, their mommies and daddies, their feelings, animals, choo-choo trains, block towers they were building and how they liked to dress up and play at home. The predominant project was *food*, and it was being taught with culturally responsive pedagogy, yet we wondered how much the children understood that there is a larger world than they were experiencing in the present moment and how they actually conceptualized the world. The teachers were questioning this notion for themselves, and they stated that they were learning with the children and their worldviews were expanding. They wanted to "learn more about what's going on in the world to be more confident in what we are teaching." Teachers were aware that the Slattery children were privileged enough to have adequate food and that there were children in the world that were without food. They were beginning to see their own classroom and teaching practice within the context of the international community.

The next project was *homes and habitats*, particularly interesting for people who are not living in their countries of origin, and also interesting for almost everyone. The subject of *home* touches into a universal archetype and human need, and therefore it was an emotionally powerful subject for the children to investigate. The project was about people and animals, and began with an emphasis on books to introduce new ideas. The teachers read a book to the children about a little bird who flies away and then comes *home,* a theme that coincides with the children's growing autonomy and separation and individuation from their parents and *homes.* The children go to school every day and then they come *home,* so they could identify with the baby bird. This was the start of the project, in the local and family environment, so that the children could feel emotionally connected with the concept of *homes and habitats.* Then they learned about turtles, who are local, and bears, who are definitely not usually local in South Florida. At that point the teachers introduced a map and globe and tried to get the children to learn the concepts of countries, continents and seas, but they met with frustration because the children could not comprehend what was not in their here-and-now environment. The children are just starting to learn about visual symbolic representation and how a visual symbol can represent something in non-present reality. The teachers concluded that they needed more interactive learning experiences, so they created with the children a bear habitat, a bird nest and an ocean environment. One of the teachers brought in a real turtle with its habitat, and the children were fascinated, asking many questions and, of course, wanting to touch everything. The teachers showed educational videos of homes around the world, and the children built their own houses with pictures of their own bedrooms, so they learned that people live in different places and have different homes. The teachers showed them a book of photos of children's bedrooms around the world and spoke about the differences and similarities to their own homes and bedrooms. The curriculum principle of moving from local to global was, once again, echoed in these important curriculum decisions. In the classroom, the children together made a big home out of a large cardboard box, bit by bit, in the dramatic play area. That home belonged to all the children in the class, a significant learning experience for children who were learning about the world and developing empathy and interrelatedness with other children. One day they painted roof tiles, and another day they focused on what goes inside the house. They played and played with the house they had invented. In the art area, one little boy painted a light blue circular picture of a globe, stating, "I paint globe. It is circle. It's blue and green." Sometimes the children and teachers used words from different languages in the classroom, and the

Spanish teacher came in regularly to sing songs about homes in Spanish and to introduce new words in Spanish. One of the mothers came in dressed in a traditional Chinese outfit, sharing Chinese dumplings with the children and teaching them the word for "good luck" in Chinese. The children did learn that there is a bigger world out there and that people live in *homes and habitats* in different ways, as well as that we should embrace, celebrate and understand differences. It was questionable how much they could actually conceptualize about other countries because other cognitive developmental tasks took precedence for the most part. Children's learning was uneven and made us wonder, but the teachers felt it was essential to persevere and lay the foundations of global competence by introducing children to the wider world. The teachers were involved in the important and challenging work of integrating global knowledge into the classroom projects, and giving children a broad view of not only *homes and habitats*, but about respect for the dignity of all people, everywhere.

Another project began on the topic of *transportation*, because the children were playing choo-choo with baby dolls and pretending to feed them, demonstrating that they were interested in the whole idea of transportation and babies, too. When the teachers initially questioned the children about transportation, they were surprised that the children knew about submarines, airboats, dump trucks and other forms of transportation. They decided to focus on transportation via air, water and land. Because the children seemed to be visual learners, they included pictures of different boats, and the children talked about boats they had been on, not an unusual experience for children in South Florida. A teacher who was from Alaska taught the children about fishing boats and her family's boat in Alaska. Almost all the children had never heard of Alaska before then. They learned the parts of a boat and then constructed a sailboat, with new vocabulary words for parts of the boat. One day the teachers took the children into the parking lot to observe and talk about cars, and they sat in a car in the driver's seat, learning all the parts of a car, like the steering wheel and the dashboard. Inside the classroom, they constructed a cardboard box car and painted it blue, placing it in the dramatic play area for the children to interact with. The children even included homemade license plates with numbers on them. For outdoor play, the children made stoplights, with red, green and yellow pretend lights, that they used to regulate traffic when they played on tricycles. And then a wonderful, teachable moment occurred. The teachers reintroduced the globe, but this time they decided to use the concept of near and far, and they made a friendship map, the first of its kind in our school. With the map, they spoke about how to get from one person to another and made lines to connect people on the map. Through conversations with the children, they began to explore, for example, how to get to someone's grandmother's house in a different country. Then they referred to transportation around the world and what was available. One of the teachers was from the Philippines, and she shared that in her country, people get around by riding on elephants. The children loved that idea and asked to learn more about elephants. They constructed a rather sturdy elephant that the children could sit on in the dramatic play area, and that elephant is still there today. It became part of the classroom, and it was made to last. The teachers were successful with this conceptualization of internationalization because they had built the groundwork with the children, and because they designed the activity based on the children's family networks and experiences. The teachers were learning with the children about how to internationalize curriculum for three-year-olds.

The Older Three-Year-Old Classroom

This classroom was markedly different from Slattery's other three-year-old classroom. The children were a bit older and developmentally a little bit more advanced by several months, in general. However, the teachers were having an extremely difficult time accepting the idea of internationalization in the first place, and they wanted specific directions about how to do it. They did not seem willing to take risks and be adventurous with new creative ideas, and they did not recognize the value of global competence for young children. In addition, they were also not working well together as a teaching team, with a lack of structure and organization and a confusion of boundaries and expectations among co-workers. This sometimes happens in early childhood schools, and the director's intervention may become necessary. Throughout the first year of Slattery's curriculum internationalization process, there were classroom observations conducted and directions for classroom management and organization agreed upon by the teachers through written classroom teaching contracts, to avoid any ambiguity. Teacher dissatisfaction and poor classroom teaching team collaboration was an impediment to the internationalization process, and it was very real. It was questionable if any progress would be made by this classroom, and we questioned whether the interpersonal skills and dynamics of people working together would actually be resolved. The director and I were determined to persevere, and I made several classroom observations, to help set priorities and recommend effective teaching strategies for project-based curriculum.

The first project that the children were working on was about *space*. It was questionable how this project was decided upon, and the implementation of the project appeared to consist of several disconnected activity ideas in what looked like day care and not early childhood education, with intentional teaching in a project-based curriculum. There were globes representing planets hanging from the ceiling, books read to the children about the planets and snowflakes, and moons made out of modeling clay. The children made spacesuits with the American flag on them. They played interactively in dramatic play, in the block area, and outside in the garden. The children made a play garage in blocks and brought in items from home for show and tell. There was a world map on the wall, but it was rarely referred to. During story time, the teacher introduced the idea of an astronaut control panel and patch by reading a book about it, and she told the children they could visit the solar system. The children did an art activity about constellations and learned that new vocabulary word. They made a spaceship in the dramatic play area and played astronaut with enthusiasm on an almost daily basis. The children did not act out any global play themes in their spaceship and didn't seem to understand that it would go above the whole world, even in their imaginations. A lot of time was spent making Christmas decorations during the holiday, like candy canes and paper snowflakes. In outdoor play, the children played patty-cake, karate, Ninja Turtles, looking for treasure, and making a hideout. In dramatic play, in the classroom, they briefly mentioned a rocket ship, and then went on to play elevators and enacted the big, bad wolf. It seemed like the children were not intellectually challenged within the project of *space* because there was no carry-over into their play behavior. The classroom seemed disorganized and confusing. A meeting with the teachers resulted in identifying several languages and cultural backgrounds of the children, including Turkish, Bulgarian, Russian, Spanish, Norwegian and South Korean. The other children were from families that spoke English at home. Although we brainstormed about teaching strategies to implement culturally relevant learning practices, there was little actually accomplished as this project concluded.

A change in teaching staff occurred, with the lead teacher retiring and the assistant teacher becoming the lead teacher in the classroom. The shift in teachers made a huge impact on the quality if the curriculum and on the teaching team because the new configuration of teachers were able to work together effectively. This can happen when there is a staff change in any early childhood school. There is usually an adjustment period while teachers get used to new roles and responsibilities, and that was certainly the case at Slattery. The teachers were able to formulate a new project based on the children's interests, and that project was the *rainforests*. They started by focusing on the Amazon rainforest and intended to extend to rainforests in other continents as the project evolved. Children made a collage of the animals they thought lived in the rainforest, they drew the rainforest and constructed it in manipulatives. A world map was on the wall and it became part of the children's daily conversations. Parents came in and shared that their children were constantly talking about the rainforest at home, and they wanted to learn more, resulting in parents asking how they could support children's learning. The director helped to locate additional learning materials about the rainforest, and basically, everyone was enthusiastic and involved. With the help of their teachers, the children created a multi-layered rainforest in the hallway of the school, so all their friends in the other classrooms could see what was happening. Bit by bit, the children made the layers, with rocks and pebbles, and real moss. They made little clay animals to place in the corresponding levels where they lived, and they added leaves in the layers, too. They understood that there were rainforests around the world, and trees. A child's mother who was from Brazil came into the classroom and presented on the Brazilian rainforest, incorporating the international perspective from within the population of children and parents, so she had an audience of children who were absolutely fascinated. The teachers created a book based on this experience and incorporated Portuguese words. The children then voted on which animals they wanted to study, and they selected toucans, to everyone's surprise. They knew that toucans lived in the rainforest, but the teachers wondered why the children were so interested. It turned out that the toucan image was used in advertising, on cereal boxes and cookie boxes. The children and their parents conducted a toucan search in the local supermarket, documenting toucan pictures, and also pictures of monkeys and eagles. In the classroom they read a book about a kapok tree, and the children explored nature items that were local, and viewed international videos of rainforests, to compare natural rainforest environments. They actually visited the local Palm Beach Zoo, and the teacher also read them a book about children and rainforests around the world. This project was successful because the teachers followed the children's interests, involved the parents, and worked together to create an integrated project on rainforests.

The teachers were more confident about identifying the next project, *cities,* and they recognized that the children had previous learning experiences about local and global knowledge. Therefore the project became complex and broader in scope than in the previous project. Teachers understood that they needed to start with a local context and then build into the global extensions of knowledge. The teachers were able to identify their own cultural backgrounds and families of origin, including Canadian, Jamaican, Chinese, Puerto Rican, Cuban and American. They knew that the children's families came from almost 14 countries and that eight languages other than English were spoken in the children's homes. This was truly an international population of children, families and teachers, and they had a heightened awareness of cultural differences and similarities and their own identities. The teaching team acknowledged that internationalizing the early childhood curriculum was developed as children moved from project to project, and age level to age level classroom. The children demonstrated that they were developing global competence because they were aware that knowledge is both local and global.

The *cities* project began in the block building area of the classroom, where the teachers noticed that the children were vigorously constructing buildings and roads, and they engaged the children in a conversation about what they would like to study. Finally one little boy said, "Why not just *the city?*" and that was an enlightening moment in identifying the topic. The idea of cities was extremely popular with the children and families because several of the parents and grandparents had lived in different cities of the world, and they wanted to be involved and share their cities with the children. The children's work in the classroom started with discussions about other countries, their experiences being on airplanes, and learning different languages. They investigated stop signs outside the school and the adjacent roads, made their own stop sign drawings and looked at a South Korean stop sign with Korean words. They learned to count some numbers in Norwegian. The classroom's documentation board was on a map of the United States, and maps became something children were increasingly familiar with. By reading books about cities, the children learned that there were skyscrapers in cities, so they constructed a huge cardboard skyscraper in the classroom, made of boxes collected from members of the school community and painted it as well. The children wanted to know what is above the skyscrapers, so they made pictures of clouds that they hung above the skyscraper, on the ceiling. They knew there were clouds in cities around the world. Parents brought in photos of different cities, which were displayed in the classroom. The children's appetite for new learning was intense, and the teachers capitalized on their curiosity.

Conversations with the children centered on what people do in cities and what is really in cities. They wanted to know how cities work. The teachers decided to make an interactive city map with the children, on a flat foldable cardboard that the children painted with roads, including a beach because our city has a local beach. They made white lines in the centers of the roads and made their own neighborhoods, with different-sized small boxes painted, representing buildings: the candy store, McDonald's, their houses, a high school, their own school, restaurants, palm trees and Burger King. The buildings fastened to the board with Velcro, so it was easy for the children to move the buildings around. They felt empowered and creative, and they played at city planning, making decisions daily about what goes where and why. Their ability to think through the locations of buildings and neighborhoods seemed cognitively advanced for three-year-olds, and they continued to astonish their teachers, the director and their parents. They added other blocks, little people dolls and street signs. They learned about the handicapped parking sign and added that. This learning activity was unique and endlessly fascinating for the children, and their engagement significantly extended their attention spans and the complexity of their thinking. Additionally, they were collecting "data" from their world and life experiences, and they were creating the new knowledge into something unusual and uniquely theirs. The teachers helped them make homemade books about the street signs, with their drawings of railroads, palm trees, and skyscrapers. Books were increasingly important, and then one day the teacher read a book about Curious George who went to the city. The children loved this book and took turns taking the book and the Curious George doll home for their families to take George out on an adventure in the city. They brought back stories and photos, and the teacher incorporated George's visits with each child's family into a classroom book. The book was then copied and sent home with each child as a learning activity extension into the home, resulting in closer bonding of the children and families in the classroom.

The interest in this project was outstanding and contagious, and it led the teachers to ask what they could do to further enhance the children's learning and how they could help the children make the connection from local to global. The teacher spoke with the director and myself, and we examined several possibilities. We recognized that the children were interested in who is in charge of cities, so we supported them in exploring who the mayor is and what the mayor does. They learned that there are mayors in charge of cities, and together they planned a trip to the local mayor's office. The teachers discussed with the children who's in charge at home, at school, in the state and in the country, and in the city. Children were prepared for the visit to the mayor's office by investigating the mayor's website and formulating questions in advance to ask her, with the help of their teachers. We were amazed at the questions the children invented and how readily they understood the idea of internet research. The classroom teaching team and parents were happy and anticipated an interesting visit. On the actual day of the visit, the children were welcomed into the mayor's office, and she was warm and gracious, showing them her desk, the photographs and awards, and her books. They took a group photograph with the mayor. Then she invited the children into the council room where they saw the seal and flag. They sat quietly until they had a chance to ask their questions, for example, "What are you doing for the city? Do you ever get mad? How do you protect the city? How do you make things better?" She answered them patiently and calmly, in child-friendly simple language which they could understand. When they returned to their school and classroom, they debriefed on what they learned and what they thought. Interestingly enough, the teachers seemed to learn almost as much as, if not more than, the children. Many of them had never interacted with a mayor, and they learned a major lesson in government and civics through this experience. Seeing local government through a real experience is powerful and something that the children, teachers and parents will long remember. The teachers reflected that global citizenship learning starts with local citizenship, and visiting the mayor's office provided direct experience and authentic local knowledge.

Back in the classroom, as the *cities* project continued, parents, other teachers, and the director, came in and shared about different cities they had lived in. After the "expert" parent visits, posters of each country and city were displayed in the classroom for the children to revisit and reflect upon. For example, one of the parents came in and presented about the city of Astana, the capital of Kazakhstan. She showed a map of the country and explained that we get there by plane, but they also have boats and trains. The children responded to her questions from their own experiences and cultural contexts. The parent showed them a flag of the country and pictures of nature, with lakes, mountains and rivers, and their houses called yurts. When she showed them the currency from Kazakhstan, one of the children thought it was an American dollar. She showed them food, especially the milk, which was interesting to the children. They were confused when the parent told them that in Kazakhstan the milk comes from horses because here in the United States it comes from cows. She showed them some festive clothing, musical instruments and ornaments, accompanied by the nouns for these items in her native language. When she asked the children for questions, they wanted to know about food, and she answered vegetables, meat and soup, which they could relate to. Then one of the children asked if he could get there by a rocket ship and thought he could get a "cool rocket ship". Another child wanted to know if they have schools there, and she answered. It was somewhat confusing to the children, but they were learning that other cities exist in the world, although it may be challenging for them to totally conceptualize what they haven't experienced directly. They were learning, though, that people in the world have similarities and differences in the ways they live, and to accept and respect everyone. The parent felt included, respected and valued, as did the other parents who shared about their cities. This created a sense of togetherness and community that strongly undergirds children's growing global competence.

In morning meeting, the children expressed an interest in garbage trucks and workers who clean up cities. They drove trucks repeatedly in the block area and dressed up as city workers in dramatic play indoors and outdoors. The children voted and decided to make trucks and cars. The teachers asked parents to bring in large boxes, and they made wearable cars and trucks that fit over them, so they could pretend to be garbage trucks. They played together in their own trucks and cars, and they enacted a great conclusion to the city project, taking civic responsibility for pretending to keep the city clean. They were actively playing at citizenship, by taking roles to be integral parts of their community. Teachers were proud that the children had learned to make decisions by voting, another step in learning about citizenship. The teachers remarked that they had become more open-minded and willing to learn, and they felt closer to the parents because they had incorporated the parents' cultural experiences into the classroom curriculum. They were learning with the children, and the parents were learning from each other. We all understood, once again, that curriculum is something we all do together as a community in our school.

Four-Year-Old Classroom

Four-year-olds have developed increasingly complex language and cognitive skills, and they are continuing to learn about social behavior and relationships. They have a larger fund of vocabulary, know some descriptive language, and are able to express their needs and use language for social interactions. Cognitively, they are beginning to understand cause and effect, sequences and planning, time and the interconnectedness of ideas. The children's attention spans continue to increase and, therefore, classroom projects are complex and last longer, sometimes for the whole year. They are beginning to recognize and articulate similarities and differences in appearances and in functions, and they can categorize visually and conceptually as well. Children ask questions and revisit their tentative hypotheses about how different aspects of the world function. They have a sense of self, are able to focus their attention, can usually delay gratification and wait their turn although with difficulty, and can identify their likes and dislikes and their growing awareness of their cultural backgrounds. Socially, four-year-olds have learned to take initiative and hopefully to take risks, and they are trying to figure out the social rules of behavior, making friends, and seeking out adults for comfort and security. In the United States, they generally leave their early childhood schools and move on to the "big boy and girl schools" when they are five years of age. During the four-year-old year of schooling, they are psychologically preparing to leave and go to a new school, and they are aware of this throughout the year. They are therefore under pressure to learn their "ABCs" and to write their names and letters, which is required in more formal schooling. The state of Florida provides a free tuition Voluntary Pre-K (VPK) Program for three hours per day, with its own set of standards and goals that must be followed in order to receive funding. Therefore, both of our four-year-old classrooms at Slattery incorporate VPK standards into our project-based curriculum, which complicates the internationalization of curriculum process. A global early childhood curriculum for four-year-olds must, in our setting, include the VPK standards, and the teachers have experience with integrating these standards creatively, and in ways that match their own teaching styles.

Both of our lead teachers in the four-year-old classrooms have an awareness of the world because their backgrounds are international, one from Pakistan and one from Peru. They can be described as people who teach with an awareness of the world related to world news and politics, and they are conscious of the inequities that exist across the world. They are experienced teachers and have many instructional strategies to work with the children, and they are dedicated to the internationalization process in our curriculum. We are fortunate to have teachers with these qualifications and backgrounds because their perspectives, based on their life experiences, strengthen and support the global curriculum. In four-year-old classrooms around the world, this is not always the case.

One of our four-year-old classrooms began with a project on *life under the sea,* a topic that children had experienced directly because our city has a local beach and they had all enjoyed going to the beach with their families. The classroom project supported deeper learning and identification of the layers of the ocean and which animals live there. Books were significant in stimulating the children's thinking, and the teacher read them an alphabet book on the subject of "underwater" and what it's all about. They selected the octopus as their first animal to investigate, and together they made a huge octopus and learned about the octopus' body parts, comparing the octopus to their own bodies. This was really the four-year-old version of comparative anatomy. The next animal was dolphins, and they were absolutely intrigued, creating a large dolphin for the classroom, reading books about dolphins and what they do and how they communicate. They watched YouTube videos of dolphins and learned that dolphins live in all the different oceans of the world. This aspect of global knowledge emerged naturally as part of their investigations, and they incorporated the fact that there are several oceans in a big world, not just the one local ocean that they are familiar with. That was a revelation for many of the children. While they were studying the oceans and ocean animals, they were focusing on emphasizing kindness in their classroom, and the teachers supplied a chart with their names and "kindness coupons" for kind behavior among the children. They actually signed their names on a kindness contract, so they would be responsible for their behavior, and they collectively agreed to be kind to one another. Somehow the concept of kindness extended in the children's minds to the ocean animals, and they became aware that they could and should be kind to animals, too. They started talking about our planet, and demonstrated a new way of understanding that we all live together with the ocean animals, except people live on the land. Teachers reported that they enjoyed when the children spoke about the world and their eyes lit up when they understood that they were and are part of a big interconnected world. They began to discuss keeping the oceans clean and recycling, and it became evident that they were learning about the world and also how to begin to make a positive difference.

The teachers in this classroom were from Peru, Florida and Haiti, and the children were from several countries and many had travelled to other countries to visit relatives. The teachers and the director decided to make an experiment and build on their prior knowledge, so the director brought in different rubber animals for them to play with in the block area, including a tortoise, cat and some wild animals, and the children played readily, eager to learn about how to keep animals safe and what shelters for animals are. Books were pivotal in the children's understanding, and they used books as references and as starting points for questions and discussions. Teachers hung up a map of the United States, and then the children learned from a book that there are three kinds of bears. They wanted to know what bears eat, and they drew pictures of bears and bears eating. The children made the connection between kindness and the bears, and they wanted to know how they can protect and take care of the bears. Developmentally, they were growing in their ability to empathize, and they really did care about making sure the bears in the world were well taken care of. It was at this moment that the teachers realized that the children were interested in the concept of conservation, and they designated the new project as *wildlife conservation*.

The children and teachers worked together for almost an entire year, and learned all about wildlife conservation, which spanned the globe in its exploration and discovery of animals, animal habitats and threats to the natural environment and animal habitats. Children and their parents were engaged in endless explorations, conversations and thinking about how young children can make a difference to support the animals around the world. The teachers built on the children's growing cognitive and social capacities, and they provided hands-on learning activities to enhance and extend their global learning. For example, when they learned about bears as endangered, they gave the children pieces of ice to hold and watch melt, so they could feel and observe the way bears get stranded. When they discovered that bears eat berries, they let the children smash real berries and spread it on bread, counting the berries and practicing smelling in the same way that bears smell to look for their cubs. They watched as the ice melted away and the bears would lose their homes. The children were able to articulate what they knew about animals, and that became the starting point for their next learning explorations. The children made statements such as: "Some animals run slow and some run fast. Hey, all have bones and blood and oxygen. Elephants eat and have a big trunk. Monkeys can climb trees and eat bananas. If an elephant sat on you, you would die because it is big. Cheetahs run fast. They eat crabs." They wanted to know what they can do to protect the animals and how they are different from the animals. Their questions were based on what they knew, and it was obvious that they wanted to know more. Some of their favorite animals were flamingos, tigers, sharks, black bears, lions, gorillas and dolphins. Teachers used YouTube videos to show the children the different habitats that exist around the world, including savannahs, the arctic and the rainforest. The class visited a local wildlife sanctuary to see how they take good care of the animals, and some of the parents joined in on the trip. In dramatic play back in the classroom, the children played feeding the kitties, and basically taking care of the babies and animals, and each other. They built together a home for the animals in blocks, saying that "we need to do it together". Outdoors, the teachers helped them make a walkway for the bears with the outdoor blocks. The children demonstrated their understanding by playing out the themes they were learning, and expressing their knowledge of the animals in their conversations with each other. Internationalization was truly embedded in their daily classroom curriculum, and it was integrated and emerged from the children's interests.

The four-year-olds continued to be extremely interested in *wildlife conservation* around the world, and they especially cared about protecting the planet, so the teachers showed them a video on what happens if our planet gets overrun with plastic. They learned about recycling and that they could and should take responsibility for recycling. They learned the idea of advocacy, of making life better for everyone by sharing information and taking action. The children initiated a recycling activity in their classroom and it extended to the other classrooms in the school, helping the other children learn about recycling in their classrooms. They identified with signs different garbage containers and boxes for plastics, paper and food trash. Using recycled pizza boxes, they created unique dioramas of the three habitats they had studied, with paper and paint, pieces of foam, cotton, sticks and leaves they had collected, plastic animals, and homemade clay items to represent the earth. After studying so many animals that live in the habitats of the world, the children made signs to protect the environment, created art, and expressed their thoughts individually. Some of their comments were, "Don't waste toilet paper, save the trees for giraffes. If we don't protect all the animals, they will be gone. Take an airplane and go to Alaska and look for snow, then you can take care of the bears. We can build habitats for them and plant more trees and berries. We could cool the sun down with a fan. Protect the animals from scary things." Clearly, the children were learning global knowledge and to take responsibility for making positive changes. They also created a mini-museum in their classroom based on their own ideas, with recycled art. Examples of their recycled art and their ideas included a playground for a bird, a rocket ship, a Taiwanese musical instrument and a model of "the school I'm going to." Their constructions were extraordinary, boldly created without interference and shared with other children in their class. These art objects remained on display and were, indeed, evidence of children's empowerment and creativity.

The teachers reported that they were researching vigorously, almost on a daily basis, to keep up with the children's interests. They learned more about the world than they ever thought they would and were proud of their new knowledge and of the children's accomplishments and development. They said they had grown in their own "global consciousness". They liked that the children were having conversations about the world in school and at home, as the parents shared what the children said. The children were identifying global problems and inventing solutions together, and this was a major achievement in internationalizing our early childhood curriculum. Teachers felt that they were definitely educating our future global citizens, and were becoming better global citizens in the process. The excitement was palpable because the teachers of the younger children came into the class-room to sneak a peek at what the four-year-olds were doing. They gained the perspective that what they were doing with the younger children would lead up to these kinds of developmental gains in global competence and the beginnings of global citizenship. It was an inspiration and catalyst for the teachers of the younger children.

The Other Four-Year-Old Classroom

Slattery's second four-year-old classroom engaged the children in fascinating and educationally rewarding classroom projects as well, and also served as a definite inspiration for the other teachers in the school. The group of chil-dren were particularly verbal and energetic, active learners with a great deal of curiosity and enthusiasm. They needed to spend considerable time out-doors expending their energies so they could come back to the classroom and focus their attention. Classrooms at Slattery previously had included family holiday traditions, and this class was no exception. They read a book on traditions around the world, referring to the children's families of origin. Teachers were encouraging kindness and praised the children when they were gentle and kind with one another. They made Christmas cookies, talked about Santa, trips to see relatives, and learned about Chanukah and Eid. The children were introduced to the globe and were read a book about children from all over the world, comparing similarities and differences, and they discussed how every child is special. It became apparent that this group of children knew there was a wider world than their local environment. However, it was challenging to identify a topic for the project. In the previous project, they demonstrated a fascination for different kinds of art from around the world. The teachers decided to expose the children to a new art form, Rangolis, originally from India, and created by the children with sand on small canvases. They made engaging and very colorful designs with small heart-shaped images, so beautiful that many of the parents asked to take them home and into their offices at work. The Rangolis were a source of pride for the children and they wanted to know more. One of the most cheerful Rangolis made by the children was displayed near the entrance to the school for all to enjoy.

The teachers inquired of the children what they knew about art around the world. They were a talkative group and spoke spontaneously on a range of diverse topics, such as Ninja Turtles, helicopters, the movie *Frozen*, iPhones, baseball, chocolate, cookies, superheroes, gummies, pinatas, airplanes, castles, spacesuits, food, flying and animals. Then one day the teachers observed them building with great enthusiasm and complexity with the blocks, and they pretended to be Ninja Turtles fighting, so the teachers intervened and spoke to them about who Leonardo Da Vinci really was, and they listened. Several of the Ninja Turtles are named after artists. Later, the teachers read the children a book on who Leonardo Da Vinci was, and they were quite attentive; they wanted to know more and were astounded that Da Vinci was a real person and not a Ninja Turtle. Da Vinci became a subject of study and the children explored his sketches of buildings, and learned that he was an architect. They learned about his life, and his values, especially how he loved to paint, draw and create buildings. They were fascinated and began questioning how buildings get made around the world.

The teachers built on the children's interest and helped the children learn about Brunelleschi's cathedral in Florence, Italy. They began to investigate the cathedral, and so a new project topic was identified, *art and architecture of the world*. It became apparent that the teachers were just as excited as the children about this project. Every day they came in with new questions and challenged the children and themselves. The children were also learning about world history because the cathedral was built in Italy so many years ago. Children were indirectly learning to see themselves within the context of history, in terms of the past and present understanding of themselves moving through time. Constructing a replica of Brunelleschi's dome was a challenge for the children, and the teachers empowered them to solve the logistical issues as they actually created the dome. They learned new vocabulary such as circumference, estimation, comparison, blueprints and octagons. They wanted to use clay and wood, and cardboard, too, and then one little boy suggested to "stuff it with paper" to make the dome. Little by little, the dome was constructed with the foundation and the rest made of paper mache, with one task after the next, day by day, so the children learned perseverance and problem solving for complex constructions, along with geometry and measurement. This process included making the stained glass rose windows out of colored tissue paper. They felt like architects themselves and eagerly talked about Brunelleschi's dome in Italy to anyone who visited the classroom and asked about it. In fact, it was hard to get them to stop talking about it because they were so engaged and excited about what they were learning. Some of the children spoke about how they didn't have computers in those days or videos, and they tried to figure out how Brunelleschi did it, demonstrating their growing awareness of the thought processes of others, including those who lived in the past.

The international aspect of this project was almost taken for granted because it was so natural in the children's understandings. The fact that it was in Italy was just that, a fact about the cathedral being in another country and they understood that. It was obvious that the children had somehow internalized an international perspective without having to be to be reminded. This may have been due to their experiences in the past year in the three-year-old classroom while we were beginning to internationalize our curriculum. Parents got involved more than in previous years, almost without being asked because the enthusiasm was so contagious. With a parent's help, the next activity with the children was the creation of a Korean palace, and it began with a parent teaching the children the art of calligraphy. They experimented with black ink and brushes, taking risks and experimenting with new art materials. Children naturally comprehended that in different parts of the world, there are different kinds of art and writing. The children then constructed a magnificent and extraordinary Korean Temple out of painted cardboard, carefully planning the building with their teachers. The roof of the building consisted of painted cardboard rolls to represent the roof tiles, and there were open spaces in the front for the door and windows. When I asked a little boy to tell me about it, he described the structure, but when I asked what people actually do in there, he said, "They play!" Four-year-olds think about play a lot, and I was glad to see how he could incorporate this important aspect of his own development with the global and creative experience of constructing the Korean Temple.

The project of *art and architecture of the world* seemed endless and involved everyone: children, teachers, parents and the director. Everyone was eager to bring the world into the classroom, and to invent activities to actively engage the children. Another parent, originally from Peru, brought in artistic artifacts, a retablo ayacuchano and some Inca pottery, and explained the significance to the children. We found some pieces of wood in a local store and the children created small clay figures they painted and glued into place to make their own retablos. These were displayed for all to see, and when people visited the classroom, the children were able to explain what they made and what country it was from. Through their artwork, they had learned about the world and how the visual arts reflect different cultural ideas such as storytelling and the lives of everyday people. Through story books, they learned about the Inca Trail and proceeded to make their own version of Machu Pichu, constructed out of clay on flat cardboard boxes. They were able to confidently take risks and solve problems related to the process of creating buildings, in their roles as architects. When I visited the classroom, the children told me stories about the Incas, who they were and what they did. Again I witnessed that the children had become global citizens through their deep immersion in global knowledge, and by the teachers and parents sharing a perspective of the world that included all countries and all people. Teachers and parents were learning together, too, and serving as global role models for the children. Teachers reported that they learned many fascinating things about global cultures, and they wanted to keep learning. They said that the children were learning, in their words, "cultural empathy and intercultural fluency". The teachers also emphasized that the children were learning that people are more similar than different, and that the differences are to be celebrated.

The next project in this classroom was on *peace*, and it contained several elements of curriculum that were noteworthy. It was a project that somehow got the attention of the entire school, and teachers from other rooms came in to the classroom regularly to see what they children were learning. The results of this project became evident in the children's drawings, described and analyzed in the Chapter 5 of this book. Teachers reported that they were amazed at how the children think and formulate inquiry questions. Teachers were surprised almost every day at how the children would learn and form new knowledge which seemed rather abstract, cognitively, in ways we previously had not anticipated. They were repeatedly surprised at how far children can go in their thinking when adults follow their lead and don't limit them. We noticed that the children connected their learning concepts from one classroom project to the other, too, because their memory skills were increasing along with their ability to recognize and talk about the interrelationship of ideas. Four-year-olds are in the process of learning how to get along with each other, from a developmental perspective, so the project topic of peace was a natural fit with their social development.

The project began with the teachers initiating a conversation with the children about citizenship, and what it means when people live and work together. Rights and feelings emerged in the conversation and the children spoke about sharing and kindness. Teachers asked the children for their own definitions of peace and rights, and their responses linked their global and local knowledge. They referenced the globe and learned that citizenship is a global concept; there are citizens in different countries and continents in the world and they all live together, hopefully in harmony, on one planet. Activities to help children understand these ideas involved the children making musical instruments and learning to play music together in an orchestra. They made their own pretend guitars that they could play and one of the parents who was from Australia came in and played a digeridoo. Children quickly absorbed the idea that people make music differently in different parts of the world, and they asked many questions and studied the map of the world.

At the Christmas holiday season, the children expressed their wishes to help other people in the world, and learned about caring on a personal and international level. They were introduced to the United Nations and its role in promoting world peace and the rights of all people. Sensitively, the teachers shared some of the world problems, and introduced the reality of privileged vs. underprivileged populations. Children understood and talked about issues such as some children not having schools in the world, and people not having clean water. The children wanted to help; it was obvious that they had learned that we are all responsible for each other. One child said, "Peace is food for everyone." They constructed a United Nations building in the classroom, complete with different country flags, all made by the children. The school's director helped the teachers locate children's books on this subject and they read several meaningful books to the children. The goal was for the children to understand that they are citizens of the classroom, school, neighborhood, state, country and world. These themes were reflected spontaneously in children's play themes, and parents reported that the children discussed these topics at home.

The children planned and initiated their own peace rally on the campus so they could talk with students and faculty about peace and what it is. In this way, they were definitely learning to take action and to be real citizens of a community. They made placards with slogans about peace and invented a series of questions to ask the adults. The teachers were shocked and in awe of the level of the children's thinking, and their ability to empathize and listen to other people. They had exceeded the developmental norms for their age and were actually educating the adults who came by to talk to them. It is surprising and indeed refreshing for young four-year-olds to be asking adults about what peace is and how we can promote a world at peace. On the day of the peace rally, parents came along with their children to the designated spot on the campus, and they were proud of their children, taking photos and watching the children with great appreciation. A reporter from a local television network came and filmed the peace rally, and it was on the local nightly news. This event was ground-breaking and made an impact on all the teachers in the school, and on parents and the local community. At this point we wondered if internationalizing our curriculum really was a new and modern form of peace education in early childhood.

In the classroom, a peace table was identified, which is an idea that originated with Maria Montessori, and our teachers borrowed it and used it effectively. Children learned about conflict resolution and the vocabulary related to solving problems and misunderstandings, such as compromise and collaboration. A quilt for the peace table was made by the children to further illustrate their ownership of the peace table and its purpose. It was definitely their peace table, without a doubt. The conversations continued about people working together, and the teachers introduced the idea of sports and the Olympics, where people from all over the world play sports together. Children watched YouTube videos of the Olympics and named themselves as representatives of different places in the world. They were interested in the torches coming together as one torch, and they constructed their own Olympic Torch representing the Oneness of people being united and connected. Then the class discussed the possibility of constructing an Olympic Peace City, and activities proceeded.

Throughout this project, the teachers in this classroom were distinctly changed and their comprehension of the countries of the world profoundly shifted and expanded. They reported that they learned to be aware of the causes and problems in the world, and that nothing happens in isolation, we are all connected. The teachers learned from the children how intensely powerful a classroom project can be, and that the decisions we make every day can ultimately impact on the world and its people. I watched them grow in their sense of responsibility as educators and how pleased they were with the extensive knowledge they had gained. They spoke to me about how knowledge never stops, and that seeing the children interact with the community was one of their proudest moments in their teaching careers. Their self-esteem as teachers increased and they expressed a renewed sense of the significance of their profession as early childhood educators. This awareness spread throughout the school and impacted everyone.

Postscript

The following year, classroom projects exhibited different levels of internationalization, possibly because I wasn't present as the researcher and faculty in residence, and the global committee of teachers wasn't formally organized around any specific function. The integration of global knowledge was sometimes successful and developmentally appropriate, but in other instances teachers were not as focused and determined to cohesively internationalize their curriculum projects. There was no mechanism for sharing global integration across the classrooms, and the global committee did not lead the effort.

All classrooms included Spanish integration of songs, dances, books, Spanish vocabulary related to the projects and Spanish games that were extensions of the project activities. In almost all classrooms, parents were invited in to share their cultural traditions in terms of food, holiday celebrations, and stories of their ancestors for the three and four-year-old children. The babies' classroom project was "people" and they explored where the children's families were from, with parents bringing in food from their countries of origin and also helping the children to learn about different forms of transportation in different countries. In the two-year-old classroom, the project was about weather and the teachers incorporated many developmentally appropriate hands on science experiments related to wind, rain, wind and sun. The children made a Brazilian rain stick and used it for a musical instrument, and then the teachers created a chart of cities in the world with corresponding types of weather and average temperatures. How much of this the two-year-olds understood is questionable because they are in the stage of sensory motor development and it may be challenging for them to comprehend more abstract concepts.

In the three-year-old classroom, the project was community and it was broadly defined, with different aspects of community derived from children's interest in airports and travel. Two children travelled to other countries and returned and created documentation of their trips to other communities in Germany and Austria. After that, they used a world map and added trains from around the world, and learned about destinations to communities in other regions of the world. The fact that there are other communities elsewhere and people living in them, was new learning for the children. The younger three-year-old classroom was engaged in a study of books, but internationalization was not really integrated into their activities. They had a child from Korea in the class, and the father came in to help the children celebrate the Korean New Year with food, bowing activities and traditions, Korean games such as Tuhondori, and they ate Korean sweet rice cakes. However, this was not necessarily integrated in to the extension of global knowledge and the project on books. It seemed like an extra activity. Later the children explored seaweed and were exposed to the idea of the oceans in the world, but whether they could conceptualize the existence of oceans around the world is uncertain.

The four-year-old classrooms did internationalize their curriculum projects, but the project topics were so all-encompassing that they diverged into different areas. Sometimes they went for a few months without thinking about anything international, and then the teachers inserted globally inspirited learning activities. In one four-year-old classroom, the project was on books written by the children's book author Eric Carle. The children's work had an international dimension when they began to write and document their autobiographies which included the children's heritages from other countries and locations, for example, Italy, China, Turkey, Puerto Rico and France. The children drew pictures, created maps of the location, learned about artists and architects and shared holiday traditions with their classmates, frequently with parent participation. Those were rich international learning experiences which resulted in a world map highlighting where their ancestors came from. The teachers read the children books about peace and how we can live together in a peaceful world.

The other four-year-old classroom similarly identified a broad topic for their project about geography. The title of the project then changed to "Around the World", which seemed to include the existence of everything on earth. The classroom was overflowing with documentation on all aspects of the project, and concepts such as location, relationships (people, culture and traditions), regions, landscapes and environments. Children built different houses and eventually made a map with yarn connecting children's self-portraits with the country their ancestors came from. Then the project veered off into natural resources, the history of four local cities, the map of Florida, the solar system, recycling and finally virtual tours to a nature park. The project did not appear to be integrated and internationalized because there wasn't cohesion and a framework for internationalizing children's investigations, although some of the learning activities were valuable and substantive.

During this year, however, the school's director led the teachers in creating a plan for an international children's garden to serve the entire school. This was done in a collaborative manner, with input from all the teachers working together. It was an innovative schoolwide activity that brought the teachers together around environmental issues and brought in a global perspective.

Questions for Further Inquiry: Global Competence in the Early Childhood Curriculum

The stories from the Slattery classrooms provide examples of the joys and challenges we faced in internationalizing our early childhood curriculum, to develop the foundations of children's global competence that will eventually lead to their experience of global citizenship. The majority of the time it was exhilarating, but at times it was anxiety producing when we had no idea how to continue and had to take real risks in our curriculum. At an adult level, the teachers and the parents developed their global citizenship and increased their knowledge about the world. Some of the issues we encountered may be helpful as your school develops its own internationalized early childhood curriculum. You may want to consider the following questions in your deliberations and discussions:

1 Does the development of global competence follow and match our expectations of child development and the stages of growth, or can children really learn more about the world? What do they need to know in order to form the foundations of global competence?
2 How can our classroom curriculums connect with the family backgrounds of the families we serve? How can we utilize family histories in helping young children to comprehend the world, in a way that connects with their own families and the families of their friends?
3 In what ways can we support children learning local knowledge and then making the shift to increasing levels of global knowledge? How can we help them develop and experience the interconnectedness of ideas from the local to the global, and all levels in between? What is realistic?

4 In our classrooms, at different age levels, how can we use maps (and globes) to demonstrate a wider view of knowledge across the world? How can mapping skills be taught and experienced by our youngest children? How can we then continue to develop mapping skills at different age levels?

5 Most of Slattery's classroom teaching teams experienced one or more "ah-ha" moments of revelation about the internationalization of early childhood curriculum, and how to approach it. Have you explored the subject and allowed yourselves the time, as teachers, to reflect and discover your own moments of inspiration? What were those moments? What did you learn?

6 The internationalization of our curriculum developed in the children from year to year, as the children moved up from one age level classroom to another. Have you noticed and identified how this is happening in your school? How has global competence increased in the children from year to year as they are learning about the world?

7 What learning materials have you located or invented yourselves, to match your curriculum to your specific population and location in the world? Are there books, for example, that you have found helpful and informative, or have you made your own books? The same may apply to toys, costumes, musical instruments, charts, art materials, and other learning materials. Are there nature-based materials you could use that are locally available? What technological resources might be available, to use or to share?

8 How does the cultural background of the teachers influence and impact upon the internationalization of early childhood curriculum? How might you incorporate the teachers' family histories and intercultural experiences in your curriculum? What special aspects of global knowledge might each teacher contribute?

9 How can we empower children to investigate the world? How can we help them gain courage and confidence, so they can explore and discover the world, and continue to learn about it?

10 What is the meaning of the concept of community, as children understand it, from the local to the global levels? If our world is changing and technological advances enable us to reach the whole world, how does this change what we teach young children about the experience of being an active member of their local community, and the community of people who share our world?

11 What does it mean for young children to eventually become global citizens who will take action to make the world a better place? How do we do this in our classrooms by the learning activities we provide, and by the values and beliefs we teach? At what age in our classrooms can young children identify problems and collectively begin to solve problems creatively together? How might we accomplish this?

12 How do young children comprehend the notion of economic and social privilege? What does this mean in terms of the learning activities we provide for them? How are we educating them to see and appreciate the beauty in others, and to respect and embrace their human rights and dignity?

13 How do young children's inner schemas of the world develop, and how can we help them to avoid stereotypical images of the world, and to avoid a deficit vs. privilege model? How can we support children in learning about the realities and complexity of the world and all its people? How can we counteract stereotypic and oversimplified images that are sometimes be presented in the media?

14 What learning activities can we introduce into our classrooms and communities that help children feel empowered to advocate for a better world? How can we help them to believe that they can make positive changes that impact on humanity? How do we share what the children are learning with their communities?

4 Transformational Portraits

The Teachers

Teacher Interviews

Internationalizing the early childhood curriculum is a complex process that makes changes in teachers' lives, impacting on their professional and personal identities no matter where they are in the world. Respect and appreciation of teachers' voices and their feelings, wishes, insights and ideas are essential because teachers' awareness of the world undergirds and guides curriculum for children. Children's global competence and global citizenship is directly related to how their teachers understand and conceptualize the world and how they experience the learning process as teachers of young children. Teachers' experiences contribute to the school culture and promote practical and ideational change. They need the time to reflect upon and articulate their own learning and growth, and they similarly need to feel valued and important. At Slattery, I decided this could be accomplished through a research process involving teacher interviews that gave voice to teachers and documented their experiences. However, other approaches to teacher self-expression should be encouraged and explored in any country where a global approach to early childhood curriculum is being implemented. Other methods might include discussions, paired sharing, journal writing, focus groups, videotaping and reflecting upon classroom practice.

In this chapter based on our program at Slattery, an analysis of teacher interviews provides evidence of the transformations of teacher identity and belonging in the world and the deep learning that teachers experienced as they internationalized curriculum for the children. Previous chapters described the process of staff development, the stages of internationalization of the early childhood curriculum, and stories of the curriculum projects, with all the ups and downs, successes and challenges. Initially we intended to develop global competence and global citizenship in children but after my experience as a researcher immersed in the process of extensive observations, it became obvious that there was a substantive impact on teachers and that this data needed to be collected and analyzed. It became time to learn from the experiences of classroom teachers who had experienced professional development to enhance their own global citizenship and to further their curiosity about the world. At the end of the second year of implementation, a teacher interview questionnaire was designed to gather and track this significant data.

Method

Thirteen extensive teacher interviews were conducted over a two week period. The sample included lead teachers, assistant teachers, and a floater graduate assistant teacher. They were a diverse group, including teachers with different countries of origin, a variety of age levels, different languages spoken in addition to English, a range of educational levels from the associate to master's levels, and different numbers of years of prior teaching experience with young children. Questionnaires were distributed prior to the interviews to encourage teachers to respond to interview questions with more depth and complex thinking. Recognizing that the teachers were engaged in their own development and process of identity change, and grappling with not only the content of their responses, but also with the actual creation of personal and universal meaning while they internationalized their classroom curriculums, I chose to give them time to reflect before the interviews. For many of the teachers, this was their first time being interviewed for a research project and reading the questions helped them to feel more at ease and able to respond according to their beliefs, ideas, and experiences. Interviews at the end of the second year of classroom implementation meant that teachers felt more confident in their ability to change curriculum because they had all experienced some measure of classroom successes with the children at each age level classroom.

Almost all the teachers interviewed were eager to be heard and to share their ideas, feelings, and growth process. Their attitude was basically positive and thoughtful. Scheduling the interviews was challenging because teachers were needed in classrooms. Therefore, interviews were conducted during lunch or break time and sometimes even during classroom teaching time if other teachers were available to work in the classrooms. The director supported the research and was extremely helpful with scheduling the interviews. Given the unique personalities of the teachers, some felt more comfortable with the interview process than others. A few teachers were more relaxed and articulate than others, while some teachers felt a bit awkward with being interviewed. As a researcher, I found what they didn't say to be significant as well. No one said they were bored, and no one indicated that they were stagnating intellectually. A few teachers were surprised with my neutrality during the interview, and how carefully I was listening to their responses. They were used to interactive discussions with me and had to get used to basically being the only person speaking in response to my questioning.

All 13 interviews were taped and later transcribed by me, as the researcher, and copies of the interviews were distributed to the teachers for review and cross checking. No one found any errors in the transcriptions, and almost all the teachers appreciated being given a copy of their interviews to reflect upon.

The interviews were analyzed and coded according to primary and secondary emergent themes of meaning. The three prominent primary themes were, in this order: 1) Teacher's identity as global citizens increased, 2) teacher expectations of children's knowledge changed, and 3) parent involvement increased and resulted in a stronger sense of school community. The most significant theme about teacher identity represented the largest percentage of impact, averaging at over 50 percent, with the most significant changes reported in teacher identity transformation through the curriculum implementation process. What follows is a list of the themes that emerged from the data, and a description and discussion of salient points in each theme. Teachers' voices are highlighted to illustrate the construction of meaning that teachers experienced.

A detailed list of the primary and secondary themes are as follows:

1 *Teacher's identity as global citizens increased*

   a   Resistance to change
   b   Taking risks and exploring
   c   Integrating new knowledge
   d   Excitement and awe rekindled
   e   Interconnected of people
   f   Self-reflection increased substantially
   g   Identified and appreciated the happiest and most profound moments

2 *Teacher's expectations of children's knowledge changed*

   a   Ability to not predetermine what children know and learn
   b   Openness to new possibilities in curriculum (creativity, exploration)
   c   Global learning goes on endlessly

3 *Parent involvement increased and resulted in a stronger sense of school community*

   a   Parents felt more welcome, valued and happy
   b   Internationalized curriculum enhanced the experience of community
   c   Culture of busyness influenced the school community

Teachers' Identity as Global Citizens Increased

Resistance to Change

This secondary theme was the most significant, with approximately 84 percent of the teachers commenting on their resistance and reactions to the curriculum change process, and three teachers of the 13 stating that they had no resistance at all and that they embraced the concept of globalizing their curriculum. They all seemed happy and actually relieved to be able to talk with a neutral person about their experience. Resistance to curriculum change is generally something that teachers experience, especially when they are not given a predetermined roadmap of what to do and they are expected to collaborate and create a new approach or curriculum expansion. The age level of the children made a difference, too, with teachers of the younger children doubting that this was possible, and the teachers of the older children more willing to try to figure out how to make it happen. With uncharted curriculum territory, resistance was expected and not criticized, but rather acknowledged as their experience.

Only a few teachers *embraced the idea* right away. With a large, beautiful smile and enthusiastic tone of voice, one teacher told me how great she thought this approach was and that children need to understand the world and everyone in it. She was unsure about how to apply international curriculum to her two-year-old classroom; however, she believed immediately in the idea of developing global competence. Another teacher said how she appreciated the opportunity to reflect upon what international would mean for her four-year-olds and how they would "grasp the concept that there are people around the world, and create an awareness that even though we're different because we speak a different language, we can have different features in our physical appearance, we're all humans". She believed that the children do understand and accept what global is and "what it is to acknowledge different parts of the world." Another teacher mentioned how proud she was for Slattery doing this because we were proving that the global concept could work in a school for young children, and that this was innovative and timely as a global trend in education. A teacher said that, "I think it's very important that our children at a very young age understand what it means to be part of the entire world, what it means to be global and what the world is." The teachers who strongly supported and promoted the internationalization of curriculum influenced others about what was possible as the curriculum process progressed. Therefore, in some instances, the new ideas were contagious among teachers as peers.

The resistance to change in the curriculum was experienced by the majority of *teachers who resisted change in general* and seemed to be somewhat rigid in their thinking, based on their personalities and habits of classroom teaching. Surprisingly, the teacher who was so proud of this innovative approach in early childhood curriculum described herself as needing to get out of the "safe zone". She described her experience in the following way: "Should I grow myself in a different way? Should I? So that was my struggle, so I became more creative. That was my struggle." She was able to recognize her own resistance and she was willing to move past it in new ways. The teacher of the three-year-olds initially completely dismissed the international idea, stating that she honestly had mixed feelings. She spoke about children needing to learn about their local communities before learning anything else and she viewed local knowledge as if it was in opposition to the globalization of curriculum content. Her first reaction was to oppose the global idea. A different teacher of three-year-olds struggled with her own experiences, growing up in a single culture environment and moving to our South Florida location where she experienced unanticipated groups of people from diverse backgrounds. She had been adjusting to that, and to make it more challenging, we had added the international dimension to curriculum. This was extremely challenging for her, but she somehow found a way to welcome the opportunity to reflect on her own resistance to internationalizing the curriculum, which represented another change and definitely growth for her. It should be noted that the actual amount of change a person is encountering may influence how quickly and effectively classroom curriculum change is embraced and developed. People have their own coping strategies for dealing with changes, and many react with resistance at first. Another teacher reacted by mentioning that although the children were learning that there are different languages, she was doubtful that she needed to go beyond what they had already been doing in their classroom, for example, by celebrating holidays from different religious and cultural groups to expose the children to different foods and rituals. She understood that internationalization was only about diversity education and that she didn't have to do more than she was already doing. Defensiveness is frequently a response to change, and for this teacher it was how she expressed her resistance.

Several teachers *did not believe that young children could learn international concepts*, and that became a large part of their resistance. They believed what they had been taught previously, most of them educated in Western systems of teacher education, where child development was presented in a limiting framework that represented what children learn at specific stages chronologically. They had been exposed to learning standards for children that were national and statewide, but not global. Although they had extensive staff development days about global citizenship and global competence, these were really novel concepts and created cognitive dissonance for many. One teacher said that "This isn't typically taught in early childhood. Children need to be aware of there being communities outside their own... It was difficult at first because it was so new so it was difficult to incorporate it." One teacher had never travelled outside of the United States, and her worldview was centered in the United States. She said she was not international and didn't believe that children needed the international perspective, and she questioned how young children could possibly learn this. Another teacher expressed her doubt to her teaching team in the classroom. The three-year-old classroom teacher described how significant she thought this topic was, but she was unsure if and how such young children could learn international concepts. She stated, "They may not be able to comprehend all of it... For the three-year-olds, you plant a seed in there. On their age level they may not comprehend in the beginning, but repetition is the key." She said that her teaching team had a negative approach at first, and it was hard for her to guide them because the children were so young and just developing language and social skills and awareness of other people. The teaching team did not see the reality of the children growing up to be global citizens in the future, and how their early childhood learning would contribute to their futures. The teachers were more focused on what they were doing instead of also thinking about why they were doing it and what the ultimate goals were in the children's development. New teachers seemed to need more immediate success with teaching and observing children's learning as they understood it, while more experienced teachers understood how global competence could possibly be built developmentally, step by step in young children.

The teachers of the two-year-olds similarly couldn't believe at first that young children could learn about the world. One of the teachers stated that

> it's a very difficult for them to understand the concept and, for example, they don't understand what a globe is. It's a pretty picture but they don't understand as much as their cousins or mommies and daddies coming from a different country. They may speak a different language at home but I don't know if they can really relate or understand it until they get a bit older.

Her initial questioning and resistance lead to detailed observations of what children could do and eventually yielded positive results in terms of curriculum development, even though the initial skepticism and disbelief was obvious at the beginning of the process. The infant teacher said, "At first I thought it was too young for my age group, but now I think it's a good thing for young children to learn about globalization." She was questioning how very young children can possibly learn about the world; however, as time went on, she gained an awareness that we start with the local context and build toward global awareness in young children. Resistance should be appreciated as a starting point for teacher development and not as something to be eradicated. The value of having teachers openly share their perspectives and resistances helps the director and staff developer to guide them, appreciating that everyone learns with their own style and through discovery, as do the children. Resistance should be appreciated as a starting point for growth and understanding.

Taking Risks and Exploring

All the teachers interviewed (100 percent) said that they took risks and explored new curriculum approaches, evidence of their willingness to grow and the fact that they felt secure enough to try out new activities in their classrooms, rather than simply relying on previous successes. Risk taking was reinforced by the director's ongoing support and this obviously made a big difference. The director's approach impacted on their identities as teachers, allowing them to see themselves as innovators and creators of new dimensions of early childhood curriculum internationalization. Significantly, they were not afraid to "fail" and used the opportunity to reflect on how the children responded to novel teaching strategies, and how they could improve their classroom practices.

The majority of teachers expressed the feeling of risk taking and of *going beyond one's own prior and present experience and knowledge*. Powerfully realizing that they had freedom to try out activities and to revise whatever didn't work was liberating and exhilarating for the teachers, invigorating the internationalization process with joy and a sense of adventure. One teacher said she saw the need for internationalizing the teacher education courses she had taken to incorporate the risk taking philosophy and develop globalized curriculum for young children, going beyond what she learned. She spoke about learning with the other Slattery teachers and how trans-formative it was for her and for them. She saw the potential for what this can contribute in the field of early childhood teacher education, and how teachers should extend their own learning to accomplish the inter-nationalization. Many teachers said they had a realization, and "ah-ha" moment when they recognized that they needed to learn more about the world in order to educate the children. One teacher described her learn-ing process as experiencing cognitive dissonance, comparing what she experienced in her own childhood to the worldview she needed to teach her children. She mentioned her prior learning about coconuts, and how that was different when she moved to Florida, and now how it is differ-ent when she teaches about coconuts in the world. She had to go beyond her prior knowledge to take a risk and teach the children differently from the way she had learned as a child. A teacher of the very young children spoke about how she took risks trying to help the children connect the topic of animals in the world to the animals they encountered in their local environment and homes. She said that she realized that she had to do something differently than she had done before. Another teacher spoke about how she had thought that internationalization was "above children's heads", but she realized that she had "taken a personal understanding of just globalization, our connections, the economy and different things, the connection between different people, and it's been interesting for me to transfer and see how that is in the classroom." She compared her own learning to what might be possible in her classroom. She went on to state that it's important "when you're teaching a parti-cular subject to really try to think outside the box and make connec-tions." A teacher of the four-year-olds powerfully and eloquently said that, "I have learned that there are no limitations in early childhood to expose them to the concept of being global… I learned that as a teacher I am capable of everything… Nothing is impossible and that children are capable of everything." Through risk taking and the freedom to explore, she learned exponentially.

Another realization that the teachers identified was *their need to know more and to do research about the world*. When they recognized that their knowledge was limited, they took the initiative to search for new knowledge. One teacher said, "I came back to the room with the knowledge I researched, to share with the rest of the staff. It also made me more animated when I was teaching the children because I had more facts on the topic." Another teacher described investigating topics on the internet and engaging in a lot of personal research, and she was pleasantly surprised at how much she learned and the phrases in different languages she also learned. She recognized that the new learning made her more effective, stating, "It was a lot of work on my end, trying to do a lot of research about it." She said it helped her to teach and to introduce global ideas to the children. Another teacher said she intentionally learned from the other teachers about the world because some of them are from different countries. Her research was interpersonal and not through online learning, and it resulted in increasing acceptance and understanding of peoples' differences and viewpoints. These teachers deliberately sought out new knowledge that expanded their understanding of global content.

Almost all the teachers *took risks in actual curriculum activities as they extended their project based curriculums internationally*. Teachers of the younger children struggled with making global learning concrete, so the children would comprehend it, and they were willing to try our new approaches. In a curriculum project on animals, the teacher learned and shared the names of animals in different languages, starting with Spanish because some of the children spoke Spanish at home. She showed the children pictures of animals from around the world, and they did art activities about the animals. In that way, she took a risk in making the curriculum content global. Teachers of the two-year-olds did projects on fire trucks and on bees. In each project they shared with the children photos and YouTube clips, when available, of bees and fire trucks from around the world, including different countries where the children's parents and grandparents came from. They wanted to give children an awareness that there are other countries and that in those countries there are differences from what we do, and there are similarities. They were teaching the children the foundations of global competence. The differences were included in photos on the children's documentation boards. In the three-year-old classroom, the teacher created a friendship map with the children, connecting their families of origin with the ides of friendship, from an international perspective. The parents brought in pictures of houses in other countries and they added the pictures to the friendship map. The children began to understand this new approach because it was related to what the children know, their families and their friends. A teacher of the three-year-olds wrestled with how to teach children the notion of distance between places in the world, and she invented a way to teach distance by how long it takes to travel by car, boat and airplane, and they compared the distances. The children were beginning to understand because she based their learning on what they already know about cars, boats and air-planes. She reported that her new method worked when she observed them playing about it in dramatic play and talking about distances. The other three-year-olds' teacher invented new ways to incorporate parents and grandparents into the classroom project by having them come in and teach the children about different cities in the world, with hands on activities in most cases. The teacher of the four-year-olds introduced the idea of earthquakes and the fact that it results in losses of property and of life, which she didn't directly tell them. She was amazed at how much the children already knew and how they spoke about what the victims of earthquakes experience and how we can help them. The children expressed empathy for other people across the world. Risk taking and a school culture that encouraged creativity promoted innovative classroom teaching and increased teacher's beliefs that they could try new activities and continue to grow and learn.

Integrating New Knowledge

A significant number (almost 70 percent) of the teachers interviewed felt they had successfully integrated new knowledge into their work as tea-chers who were creating and implementing project based inter-nationalized curriculums. Even though many questions remained about the internationalization of early childhood curriculum, they felt they had developed expertise and skill as teachers in this effort. Their responses were positive and hopeful.

Teachers said that *they had grown in knowledge of themselves*, and they were basically quite pleased about the change. One teacher spoke about how she understood herself now as out of the "bubble where I am in South Florida", and how she feels a sense of responsibility for the world. She mentioned that "citizenship isn't something I had thought about until very recently. That's been a big deal; it has changed me a lot." She continued,

> It's just been an exciting process. I've learned so much about myself. I've learned so much about the world, and I've learned a lot about what children are capable of and how deeply compassionate they can be. It's made me really excited, too.

Another teacher spoke about the changes in her teaching style as an interesting learning process that was valuable. She said,

> Just that it's been a struggle for me, personally, to think outside of this box, but I enjoy it. I have had a hard time pushing myself. But the kids are always wanting to learn more, so that helps push me forward as well. But I think it's great to see different parts of the world, something that's different from what we see here.

The teachers of the two-year-olds felt that as adults they were learning with the children. Teaching and learning had merged in their daily classroom teaching identities. One of them said that she had gained an awareness for herself that global concepts are foundational and developmental, and extremely worthwhile for people, children and adults alike. She commented that, "it has opened my eyes to many issues."

Other teachers had integrated new knowledge in terms of *how they viewed knowledge in internationalized early childhood curriculum*. A teacher of the toddlers totally believed that toddlers can learn through the internationalization of curriculum content, and her understanding of her role as a globally aware teacher had transformed. The teacher of three-year-olds said she recognized that mapping skills were essential in an internationalized curriculum and that this is learned by children incrementally and differently depending on their developmental levels. She realized that this was the beginning of geography, essential for global learning. The teachers of four-year-olds experienced changes in their understanding of children as emotional beings who could learn and express empathy and compassion. One of the teachers said, "I know that a child can learn anything, if it's child-appropriate and within the right planning and the right caring." She continued,

> I've learned that children are capable of being able to have that care and respect for others around our planet, something I didn't even question myself before – not for positive, not for negative, but I just never questioned it. So I believe in that they are capable of realizing that there are others in our planet, not in the same neighborhood, but in our planet, to care about.

A teacher of four-year-olds described her breakthrough as realizing that the world is "one big piece of land and not countries, states, and continents". She emphasized how significant it is to change the world in children's minds with new knowledge and learning experiences.

Additional instances of integrating new knowledge concerned *unanswered questions about internationalizing early childhood curriculum*. Two major issues emerged as teachers raised questions about how they integrated their new knowledge and experiences with the children. One teacher felt strongly compelled to take action but was unsure what to do. She said,

> This is not words any more. Yes, I have to take action. It's happening to my will, my effort, but we have to do this together, like involve our classroom, our school, and our community environment. So I think it's a big change.

The same teacher described how she thought and questioned how the new international knowledge the children created in their classroom projects could be shared with the community. She felt that children should contribute their knowledge to our society, but she questioned how and what could be done. We were learning that knowledge is global, so how does it get shared back to other people? That remained unanswered. The second question raised was about how and when we should expose young children to the notion of privilege and non-privilege, especially for young children who need a sense of security in the world. She wanted children to also understand ecology consciousness, but wasn't sure if they could comprehend the local to global concepts. Does helping children respect and honor their own garden necessarily translate into global ecology? If not, how can we make that happen? What kind of scaffolding of instruction might be provided for the children? As the world continues to change rapidly, she said, she wants the children to be able to successfully navigate and have resilience to effectively handle the changes, so she identified critical thinking as essential. How this gets translated into daily practice with three-year-olds would need further refinement and exploration. The teacher was grateful that she could raise unanswered questions, and not be made to feel that she had all the answers. She welcomed the exploration and discovery, and adult learning in her future with the children, recognizing that questioning can lead to new learning and knowledge.

Excitement and Awe Rekindled

It became evident after the first classroom successes with globalizing the curriculum that teachers felt enthusiastic about teaching and seemed to have more energy as they rose to the challenge. Approximately 60 percent of the teachers shared that they had become excited and that awe had been rekindled in their teaching experience, certainly a positive and welcome situation. Their heightened emotions were felt throughout the classrooms in our school. Teachers expressed this in unique language that revealed their own growth and awareness.

At least half (50 percent) of the teachers who responded noted that *they felt gratified and their emotions were heightened.* A teacher of three-year-olds said that we need to continue with a positive attitude and that building empathy in children is important in order to develop caring and perspective taking. She truly enjoys teaching children to be caring, and she said, "we should not give up; not everyone will agree with us. It's profoundly beautiful what we're doing here." Her appreciation for children's development of global competence was obvious in her emotional reaction. Another teacher stated that she saw a "glow on a child's face as she shared her heritage with others." She was so moved that she saved photographs of all the children sharing their backgrounds and remarked that "they're proud and you can't ask for anything more from a child than to be proud of who they are". This teacher felt that through globalizing the early childhood curriculum, she was helping children to learn to be "kind, to share, to understand and to accept anybody else, whatever the food they're eating, the clothes they wear and the color of their skin, the way they smell, their beliefs." She was emotional and had tears in her eyes as she described the process of teaching children to love and accept all people in practical, concrete ways. A different teacher spoke thoughtfully about how she wanted to teach global citizenship, saying that "I know I can do little things, but I think little things can make a change... You think I can change the world? At least I try something." She expressed her faith that step by step, through working with others, she can create a better world; she was extremely articulate about her feelings and sincerely felt good about what she was doing and will continue to do. Another teacher said she felt supported and validated as an early childhood teacher because she recognized the importance of what she was teaching.

Increased motivation was felt by two teachers; one of them was energized by bringing her global perspective to the classroom. She described her feelings,

> So pretty much I've seen a lot of cultures and I've seen a lot of different countries. This actually brings in how I educate other people because I am a lot more accepting of differences and individual differences. So bringing it to my classroom was very motivating for me.

The second teacher who experienced gains in motivation said she found it both interesting and gratifying to learn about different cultures and to internationalize curriculum. She commented that,

> It's also been really cool to see the impact it's had... I think it's very rewarding as you're developing curriculum to start implementing what your ideas are and start putting things together and then seeing how kids respond to it. So it's just very rewarding to see how well it works.

Some of the teachers described feeling awe at *the realization that as teachers they are part of a bigger world* and that young children could experience that, too. They liked the idea that they were contributing to something larger than their immediate environments, and that they were becoming global in their thinking about life. Literally, their worldviews were changing and that was noted by one teacher who said that her life had changed, and she was pleased about it. Dinners at her home now included the awareness that people all over the world were sitting down to have dinner and that some people do not have food for dinner. She said, "It made me more aware all the time as a person." She consciously, deliberately wanted to learn about other countries around the world, and she demonstrated the accompanying energy and enthusiasm to accomplish this on an ongoing basis. She was in awe as she described this change in herself. Other teachers spoke about how their worldview had actually expanded to the world outside their local community and nation. They understood that they could be global, national and local citizens, and that this was a beneficial shift in their consciousness, to their surprise. One of the teachers mentioned,

Globalization is extremely important, especially for yourself and others and to teach our kids that we're not the only ones in the world. There are other people who don't have everything that you have. They don't have backpacks, they don't have shoes, and they don't have clean water to drink.

Another teacher talked about how the world is changing and that we have to take a good look at how we are educating young children to become global citizens of the future. Recognizing that she viewed the world in a new light, she said, "I think outside of South Florida. So I think of the big picture and not just the little part we're in, like outside the United States." After she spoke those words, she was literally amazed and wide-eyed, and pleased at her newfound and newly articulated awareness.

Interconnectedness of People

Half (approximately 50 percent) of the teachers mentioned interconnectedness to other people in their interview responses. The process of internationalizing the early childhood curriculum made them increasingly aware of how people influence and interact with each other, in tangible and intangible ways in countries throughout the world. Some of the teachers had never previously thought about this, and the staff development we provided highlighted the subject. Although some teachers attended an international educational conference, their attendance did not necessarily correlate with their comprehension of interconnectedness around the world. Their understanding seemed to transcend the polarity of similarities and differences, and entered into the complexity of human relationships among all people everywhere, an infinite and incomprehensible phenomenon, but nonetheless important to address.

One teacher stated that we need to embrace global education curriculum because early childhood education is philosophically based on relationships, between teachers and children, children and children, parents and teachers, and teachers and community. She described a web of interrelationships that embody her essential early childhood viewpoint, and global interconnectedness was identified as part of that conceptualization. The same teacher realized that through the research we were accomplishing together, the information would be shared with early childhood professionals around the world in the form of a book. She was the only teacher who recognized this aspect of professional interconnectedness in the field of early childhood education. Another teacher stated that, "Well, we are all global citizens and what happens here and what happens in another country affects everybody... I have been learning a lot more about the world and the representation that I have in my classroom than ever before." These teachers described interrelationships as being at the core of early childhood education.

Several additional teachers commented on the interconnectedness of people, and one of them stated that, "Global citizenship wasn't a concept I'd thought about until very recently. That's been a big deal; it's changed me a lot." A second teacher said that she had children in her class from Turkey and Hungary, and she had learned about what was happening there with refugees. She could relate to this directly because the children she interacted with every day were from there. She said, "It was eye-opening in that I could put myself in a place over there. I'm not just this little person in Boca. It put me, like, overseas, thinking about them and the impact it has on him as a four-year-old." For this teacher, the interconnectedness of relationships in the world became very real when it touched the lives of the children in her class. She awoke to the fact that we are connected across the world. Sometimes one incident can spark an awareness and realization. A teacher from another classroom said that the internationalization of the early childhood curriculum had made her conscious of interconnectedness among people and that, "I feel like it changed my perspective... It's made me more aware to think about what's outside my community. It's made me go out more to find what I can experience." The teacher of the two-year-olds was eager to establish friendships for her children with children in other places because she felt that this was the only method to get children to understand that we are interconnected. She said, "Hopefully they'll have the knowledge that everyone's one and everyone's equal and everybody's accepting of others no matter what. It's extremely important." This teacher obviously valued friendships among children as a possible strategy to promote global interconnectedness and mutual understanding.

Self-Reflection Increased Substantially

More than half (55 percent) of the teachers reported increased self-reflection during the process of internationalizing the early childhood curriculum. This may be in part due to the fact that self-reflection was intentionally built into the internationalization process, with time allotted for dialogue and multiple opportunities for feedback. It was a conscious decision that I made with the director. Therefore the increase in self-reflection, as a finding of the research study, was not unexpected. What was significant was that the teachers experienced this as positive, supportive and enriching, and used the opportunities for self-reflection optimally. In fact, the interview experience was viewed as a self-reflective process for teachers because their ideas and experiences were given respect and appreciation. It is not known if this tendency persisted after the conclusion of the research process.

Increased knowledge of the world resulted in the *teachers questioning their own personal educational philosophies, and their heightened awareness of how economic privilege is not equitable in the world.* Some teachers understood that there are nuanced differences in how people in different countries experience the daily reality of economic privilege, or lack of privilege. However a beginning awareness of economic privilege became simplified in some of the teachers' minds as the haves and have-nots, with a clear distinction between these categories. They were surely reflecting on their country and the world, and what advantages economic privilege brings. Teachers demonstrated that they had taken for granted their own economic privilege because they had not previously examined this aspect of life until they had to internationalize their curriculums. One teacher spoke about how she now felt a sense of "belonging and understanding. It's bigger than I imagined, with more problems around the world. The world needs healing." She differentiated her adult learning from the children's learning by stating, "The children are innocents. I don't want them to really know what's going on." She reflected on her wish to learn from teachers in other countries, demonstrating her increased self-reflection and openness to gain knowledge about young children and teachers at the global level. Another teacher said that she thought about "teaching young children to take care of their world and everything." She explained that she had become aware that global mistakes like pollution were a global community issue, and she commented thoughtfully that, "If they know the effects of their actions, then they are less likely to do things to harm the world, people and animals." Her acknowledgement of the ethic of caring became highlighted in her teaching and she recognized the bigger, global perspective, and wanted the children to have that perspective as well.

Another teacher reflected on the significance of peace in the early childhood curriculum, particularly when a teacher is internationalizing the early childhood curriculum. She honestly and humbly stated, "We have to live together in harmony because there are many cultures, backgrounds, and we have to live together as one." The curriculum resulted in her discovering that "I had to adjust my thinking, and I had to come from a different place. I had to step back and process it, because of different cultures and home lives. I became more aware and considerate." Self-reflection increased, and she became a more culturally sensitive teacher due to her immersion in this curriculum change process. The same teacher said that she now understood the food chain of the animals, and how animals were abused and how they were rehabilitated in different countries. Her self-reflection led to her volunteering at a big dog ranch to take dogs for walks and feed them. She had gained a spirit of service through learning about animals in other countries when her class investigated animals around the world.

The Teachers Additionally Became Conscious of Their Own Limitations

A teacher of the two-year-olds realized that she needed to learn, commenting that "I think I need to experience the world. I haven't really travelled anywhere other than the United States and Jamaica... I need to be more exposed to the world to give back to the children about it, on a personal level." She described her learning and discovery that there's a "web of cultural and global influences around young children", and that this went beyond just their physical surroundings. She reflected on the fact that in different countries there are different ways to do things, and that she wanted to know more about this. Another teacher reflected on the fact that "it's forcing me to think differently about our world and what's out there. And I'm, like, curious about it now. I want to explore it and travel... and see situations, see what I can do next to help. I don't know." She similarly became conscious that there is information that she doesn't know, even though she couldn't definitively articulate what different countries are like, but she knew there was something beyond her immediate experiences.

Teachers Reflected on the Relationship of Global Awareness and Daily Learning Activities in Their Curriculum

Reflecting on her own awareness, one teacher stated,

> I don't think I would ever change. I think it's always been in my heart that the world should be like this. I think it changed the way I can let others understand it. I feel that I'm transformed to be a better person because of it.

She went on to describe her self-reflective process resulting in her becoming "more aware, more accepting, and more to make the world a better place. I smile and accept them and make them be noticed and proud of who they are." She recognized that she was laying the foundation for global citizenship by her own positive changes in personality and knowledge, and that this directly was implemented in her classroom with the children. A different teacher shared her perspective on a similar theme, but it was challenging for her to find the exact words to describe her own increases in self- reflection. She said,

> I feel that I need to understand more of cultures and of different things around the world, of different things that are going on... Just to be more aware of things going on around, and I feel if I can't wrap my head around them or understand them, I don't know how I'm going to teach that.

She struggled to express the feeling that she didn't know what she didn't know, but she realized that at this point in her self-reflective process, there was more and she was open to it. Self-reflection and transformation frequently involved the cognitive ability to hold contradictory types of information in one's mind until some kind of new construct or resolution was achieved. Changing oneself takes time. The changes that arose from self-reflective practice occurred over a period of time, and at a different pace for every teacher. Another teacher described this as "I need to start with myself. If I mean it, I take action." She concluded that "it's so simple and at the same time complex", identifying the paradox that frequently arises in self-reflective practice during the internationalization of curriculum, and results in positive and productive change. She found resolution and concluded that "it has transformed me because the children teach me."

Identification and Appreciation of Happiest and Most Profound Moments

The responses in this category represented approximately 55 percent of the teachers stating that there were definitely happy and profound moments during the curriculum internationalization at our school. *The majority of the responses related to the content of instruction and what children could actually learn.* Several of the teachers were surprised and delighted, overwhelmingly affirming their own feelings of competence as teachers of young children. The four-year-old classroom project on peace and the corresponding peace rally on campus impacted strongly on the teachers. The teacher in that classroom said she was most happy when parents came to her and reported on what the children said at home. She shared that "we are teaching or creating knowledge together, so we don't want it to stay in our classroom. We want to extend it to families." She described how parents told her that their children are talking about world peace and creating schools in other parts of the world. "I think that really makes me happy," she emphasized. The other teacher in that classroom shared her viewpoint that her joy came from how much the children had internalized and learned about peace, and how they could be autonomous and ask questions of adults at the peace rally. She said it was "exciting for me because they were building community right here on campus," and she noticed that they children did it mostly by themselves, with little direction from the teachers. They were well prepared. A teacher from a different classroom described the peace rally as amazing, and she noted that the children understood the whole concept of peace. She commented, "They really understood and took it to heart that people didn't have enough water, the children don't have enough food." This teacher gained a larger perspective on where the children in her classroom would eventually be in the years ahead, cognitively and in terms of global social-emotional awareness.

Classroom Projects and How Knowledge Became Global Were a Source of Pride for Some of the Teachers

During the project on bees, the teacher reported that she was astounded to learn that there were "so many different types of bees in different parts of the world, with different colors, different species." Her own realization was a source of happiness. She was also interested in learning about early childhood education in different countries, especially in South Africa, which we learned during a staff development day. In another classroom, a teacher identified her happiest moment as when a three-year-old used advocacy skills by learning about a children's swing from Serbia, and to design how to implement it at Slattery. She described it as "beautiful advocacy" from a three-year-old because he did a drawing of a swing by himself. He learned something from another country and was able to apply it in the United States.

The Expanded Experience of Community Provided the Teachers with Pride and Joy

A teacher shared that when the children drew and created portraits of each other, they learned to accept and love each other even though they are different. This made the teacher profoundly happy. A different teacher believed that a reconfigured sense of community was her greatest, most profound experience. She explained that it is very, very meaningful that you're teaching a child, but you're teaching "a human. It's a big, big part of the puzzle. It's a human being caring about its planet, which is a big piece of land, which is everything. There is no politics. There is no struggle." She went on to describe her classroom as a microcosm of a global community as "caring, as feeling, as fighting, as doing something for our global community, to take care of, to do, to take action, to advocate... This is us, community already." The essential notion in her framework of community was that the children had internalized it and they were international on the inside, which was her goal and made her have tears of joy in her eyes as she explained it. Because of this expanded experience of community, she was able to teach global concepts like the five oceans in the world, and the children understood.

Teachers' Expectations of Children's Global Knowledge Increased

Ability to Not Predetermine What Children Know and Learn

An overarching theme in this category was that *children can and do know more than we expect from them*, with 60 percent of the teachers expressing this in their interview responses. One teacher emphatically stated, "I have learned that there are no limitations in early childhood to expose them to the concept of being global... I learned that as a teacher I am capable of everything." She described a moment in her classroom when there was an earthquake in another country, and the children already knew all about it, even though the teacher did not consciously explain it to them. She assumed that they learned about it through the global news on television or overheard conversations among their parents. The children explained to her what an earthquake is and what it does to people. She said, "I did not have to mention infrastructure being destroyed... Children were able to express their feelings towards what's happening and their concerns... and their empathy by wanting to share, develop critical thinking, reinforcing and adapting problem solving into this current event." The teacher believed strongly that children can learn way beyond what is supposedly age appropriate, and she explained further, "It's very powerful... Nothing is impossible and that children are capable of everything." This was an exhilarating discovery on her part, enabling her to be more creative daily in her classroom, according to her responses in the interview. Another teacher was similarly surprised with her younger group of one-year-old children. She said that her philosophy had changed and that "we shouldn't have expectations of their limits. We should continue to take risks... It's worth a shot. You never know. I've seen children blow me away with what they can do." She spoke about how children can make connections when you start with the here and now, and then move out into other areas. The children saw a raccoon near the school and then learned about it, and then they extended their learning about raccoons into their home communities, where they lived. They were learning that animals can live anywhere and everywhere. The teacher said that if they had limited what children should know, they would have never attempted to help them transfer knowledge and make the cognitive connection about animals.

Children's Social and Emotional Learning Was Similarly Extended by the Content of Internationalizing the Curriculum

Teachers had previously been taught about the stages of children's social-emotional development, but they reported situations in the classroom where children clearly expressed compassion and empathy. They shared that the children were aware of the consequences of their actions at an earlier age, and that they were conscious of the feelings and perspective of other people. One teacher said that young children want to learn about cultural differences, and that "the children are very interested in each other's cultures; they want to know more about clothes, food, dance and music." This was identified by one of the teachers as important for global citizenship. She commented that she didn't actually believe that children could be global citizens, but by the end of the year they had incorporated the concepts and had done it well. They were learning global knowledge in the social-emotional context. The teacher said, "We had the 'wow' effect that kids could do this and you can see documentation in our hallway of what they achieved – their words, their drawings. And we all created knowledge. I learned a lot about children doing this." The children in her class had learned about global art and architecture in different countries that she referred to. "Our project has no limits. We teach as they are ready to take," she noted.

A teacher of the three-year-olds identified *foundational learning through autonomy, connected to social-emotional learning that is global in scope.* Citing children's autonomy as a central goal, she remarked that children can solve and resolve their own issues, as they develop language, and as they are given opportunities to accomplish these tasks on their own, with minimal teacher scaffolding. She felt that independence is foundational in helping children become problem solvers and in gaining global knowledge. Her classroom community was described as a place where they can learn global citizenship through autonomous hands on learning activities. She understood these issues to be foundational, and to planting "seeds of global citizenship". By learning to respect the feelings of others, she believed that she was setting in place foundational skills in children for the future understanding of human rights. A teacher of two-year-olds similarly described setting the foundation for future global citizenship, stating, "I can put the groundwork so they can relate to it later on in life, and I think that's the steppingstones for education." She referred to mapping skills the children were learning by making maps of where their grandparents live. In that way, she started with their emotional relationship with their grandparents, and helped children to comprehend what maps are, and that there is a larger world outside their immediate experience.

Openness to New Possibilities in Curriculum (Creativity, Exploration)

Approximately 55 percent of the teacher responses in their interviews indicated an openness to new possibilities for exploration and creativity in curriculum. They believed that children could learn more, and that previous notions of what determines curriculum content could be revisited and reformulated. They were open to new possibilities they hadn't considered and they were creatively taking chances. For teachers and children living in the technological age, this was significant. Several teachers discussed how *they were rethinking the connections between their own life experiences and lives in other communities around the world*, something they hadn't reflected on until they were immersed in the internationalization of their daily classroom learning activities. One teacher remarked that she took more creative risks in terms of explaining different locations to the children. Although some approaches worked and some didn't, she was not discouraged. She found it valuable to tell children about children in communities far away, and she tried to connect these ideas with the children's experiences in their communities. Throughout this process, she started to think about how people live in neighborhoods in other places in the world, which opened her mind to feeling interconnected as a human being on earth. Another teacher mentioned repeatedly about getting out of the local "bubble" and how speaking a second language helps to build bridges and relationships. She emphasized "going beyond" with creative activities and therefore extending her own creative options as a teacher.

Other teachers highlighted *their awareness that internationalizing the curriculum was laying the foundation for children to become future global citizens*, and they viewed this as an innovative exploration in possibilities. Intentionally, consciously making their curriculum content global in scope was valued as a creative process and exploration for contributing to global citizenship in general. A teacher of three-year-olds felt that children becoming able to express their feelings and solve their own problems were foundational skills for global citizenship, and she also noted that using primary sources of knowledge from the parents was extremely meaningful and she discovered new learning along with the children. She recognized that her creative approach had worked when she saw her former children "blossom" as four-year-olds ready to think broadly and comprehensively about the world. Reflecting with pride, she said, "The foundations worked!" A teacher of the four-year-olds said that she wanted to send children into the world with a positive outlook about relating to others, and that her creative classroom learning activities gave children responsibility for their world and or their identity as citizens. She illustrated her explorations in second language learning, teaching children about countries and continents, and reaching out to other people as sources of local and global knowledge. Teachable moments were a catalyst for her to enhance her own creative process as a teacher. One of the teachers of the two-year-olds concurred that young children really do understand other people's feelings, homes and families.

Expressing exhilaration in the discovery of new teaching possibilities, one teacher spoke about her *encounters with new content knowledge*, ideas that she never thought children would learn, and how that sparked her own creative teaching. She was open to teaching and learning that is boundless and unlimited in content for young children. It appeared that more of the teachers agreed with this position, but they were not able to articulate it in the interview process. This was obvious during the researcher's classroom observations. The newness of ideas may have restricted their ability to speak about how open and creative the children actually were.

Global Learning Goes on Endlessly

Fewer teachers responded to the interviews regarding this sub-theme, with a rate of about 35 percent. However, the teachers who did answer with information related to *ongoing global learning* did so emphatically. A teacher remarked, "Well, I think I've just started... We keep learning. We never stop." Another teacher discussed how the children were learning to live in an international community at a young age, and how significant that was for her. She said that teachers need to "continually educate ourselves about global issues and people." Reflecting on the interrelatedness of teachers and children, a different teacher said that the children keep learning and so the teachers have to keep learning. The teacher of the four-year-olds stated that teachers are role models for the children and therefore have to learn new knowledge and critically analyze it so they can integrate it into the classroom. Illustrating her heightened awareness of the world, a different teacher described the world itself as changing, and that teachers had to keep up with the changes so they can better educate the children. She mentioned that teachers similarly need to assist young children in accepting change in the world, and that this is important for future global citizens.

Parent Involvement Increased and Resulted in a Stronger Sense of School Community

Parents Felt More Welcome, Valued and Happy

An overwhelming 75 percent of the teachers responded favorably that parents definitely felt happier, more welcome and valued. *Families were identified as essential to the children's learning processes in the class-room, and stronger bonds were built between parents and teachers.* One teacher said, "I really want to have the family involved in the classroom, especially when you learn the process of internationalization of curriculum. I try to approach this through the family experience, the family background... It's not just coming from another country, but what's the relationship of the family." She placed relationships as central to early childhood curriculum and included the strong influence of family relationships. A teacher of the two-year-olds commented that "it brought us closer to the parents. They feel more welcome and happy to know that someone wants to know about them. They always light up when you ask them their customs, what they do at home, and the languages they speak." Gratification came for her as she gave parents a chance to talk about themselves and their families. A teacher in the infant classroom said that parents were excited to engage in the classroom and participate and share their knowledge. This teacher valued the parents' information because, in her words, "we can't get it from anywhere else, their resource. And we've had a lot more parent involvement and it's to celebrate not only where they're from but how the world works over there, like how they go to school, what happens in their school, do they have computers or they don't." She continued to share her enthusiasm about parent involvement in the children's internationalization of curriculum process. Her sentiments were echoed by another teacher who stated, "I think parents have been excited to see that we're incorporating their cultures in the curriculum... it's helped me form better bonds with the parents and families."

A teacher of the three-year-olds shared that the parents were appreciative that she had done research about their cultural backgrounds, and were noticeably pleased when she used words from their cultures and languages. It made a huge difference in strengthening their relationships, and the parents felt more a part of the classroom. However, there was one comment about a parent who didn't want her child to know about what was going on in their country of origin because it was negative and painful, and the parents had left that country for very real reasons. The teacher shared that, of course, she respected the parent's wishes. Some parents choose to protect their young children from suffering and other country-specific serious problems. Another teacher said that almost all parents "feel closer to you when you know their country and culture."

In almost every early childhood curriculum, the development of the child's identity is consciously supported and children are encouraged to express their feelings, preferences, and beliefs. As we internationalized our curriculum, identity and heritage were included in unique ways, depending on the age level of the children. A teacher shared her belief that closer communication with parents makes us a "huge family, we learn together as a global community and it's very powerful, parent involvement." She shared the perspective of identity defined as community together. In the three-year-old classroom, the teacher said that parents helped to communicate with the children and this was seen as a way to build the foundational identity of children as future problem solvers in the world. She felt that parents saw how technology could connect their children with other countries, and that parents recognized that their children's identity as global citizens was being constructed and internalized. A different teacher shared that parents felt ownership over the curriculum and they were inside it, not observing it on the outside. Parent involvement not only made parents feel welcome and happy, it made them active participants in the school's curriculum. As one teacher elegantly stated, "Parents and teachers were learning that, I'm part of the world and the others are part as well." The lived experience of community increased exponentially during the internationalization of our curriculum.

Culture of Busyness Influenced the School Community

Only a small percent (20 percent) commented on how the busyness of modern life influenced the internationalization of the curriculum and parent involvement. One teacher said that the busyness of her own life, with her own family and child, resulted in limitations in terms of how much parent involvement she could manage in her classroom. She wanted to do more research and plan more parent-centered learning activities, but there just wasn't time in her busy day to accomplish this. The other teacher who responded in this category shared that parents are busy and that timing of relationship building and parent inclusion is something to carefully consider. Not everyone has unlimited time to devote to participation in their child's classroom. The teachers mirrored the general atmosphere of the school, where the majority of teachers and parents are extremely busy and strive to be productive in their lives.

Summary: Transformational Portraits of the Teachers

The impact of the internationalization of our early childhood curriculum was unexpectedly deep, meaningful, nuanced and complex. Throughout the stages of the curriculum change process, and during the time teachers were creating a global knowledge base and projects for young children in their classrooms, they were profoundly changing in their own identities and how they understood themselves as teachers in a global world. In our particular cultural educational setting in South Florida, in the United States, the results were threefold: teachers began to identify themselves as global citizens, teachers changed their expectations of what children know and can learn, and parent involvement increased as did a stronger sense of school community. In other schools in different parts of the world, it is anticipated that teachers will undergo a transformational process of their own, based on the curriculums they utilize and the culture and school expectations. It is assumed that we cannot predict the outcomes and impact on teachers, however we do know that gaining a global perspective is an ongoing adventure, and that the children we teach benefit greatly.

As you incorporate a global perspective into your early childhood curriculum, allow yourself to reflect on your own learning process. The following questions are provided to assist you in growing as a global citizen as you do the rewarding and challenging work of learning and teaching young children. It is a privilege and it is definitely transformational.

Questions for Self-Reflection Regarding the Internationalization of Your Curriculum Process:

1   What do you think and feel about internationalizing early childhood curriculum?
2   What has the process been like for you, personally and professionally? Think back. How did you start? What did you learn?
3   What positive teaching experiences did you encounter during this curriculum change process? What was meaningful and transformative for you?
4   What were the challenges to implementing an international dimension in the curriculum? How were you transformed by these challenges?
5   Were you "stretched" to become more creative and to take creative risks? Describe what happened.
6   How has your philosophy of early childhood education changed? What do you believe now?
7   Internationalization may include an extended sense of community to include the global perspective. Has your experience of community changed to include the international perspective? If so, how?
8   What have been your happiest and/ or most profound moments during the internationalization of curriculum in your school?
9   What have you learned about how to make the world a better place? Explain and give examples.
10 How has your own cognitive construct/ schema of the "world" transformed?
11 How have your relationships with the children's parents changed during the process of internationalization of your early childhood curriculum? How has this transformed your understanding of relationships with parents and families?

12 During the internationalization of your early childhood curriculum, you have supported children developing global competence and global citizenship. Has your own experience of global competence and global citizenship been transformed? Explain.

13 What do you feel you still need to learn, to become more and more an educator who is a global citizen?

14 Is there anything else about the internationalization of your curriculum that has been meaningful and transformative for you?

5 Children's Voices and Artistic Expressions

Introduction

The heart and soul of early childhood education is our children, what they think, how they feel and who they are becoming in a very complex, globally connected world. This chapter explores their ideas and artistic creations during the process of internationalizing the early childhood curriculum in our school. As a researcher and teacher, I always try to include and carefully listen to children's viewpoints and do my best to understand what children really mean. Their words and visual art provide a window into their worlds and help us to actually assess our own effectiveness in internationalizing the curriculum for them. Have we been successful? What else do we need to include to help them better understand the world? Children work hard to integrate knowledge and synthesize ideas. Therefore, their stories and visual symbols reflect what they know and who they are. Each child has a unique style of self-expression, which made this part of the research both fascinating and enlightening.

Throughout the years from birth to five, children develop visual symbolic representations, and they are beginning to form visual schema that illustrate their daily lives. Children in the infant and toddler years are in the scribbling stage, and their images become more intentional while they assign meaning to their scribbles. However, the meanings often fluctuate, and the act of scribbling as a process is paramount. Because four-year-olds are usually able to draw pre-schematic images that are somewhat recognizable and stable, even in a rudimentary form, this research focused on the artwork and accompanying stories and explanations from our four-year-olds. At this age level, the children were able to express meanings that were increasingly consistent during the pre-schematic stage of artistic development. Usually drawings of people were some of the first schematic images the children created. Their visual artwork corresponded to their assigned meanings and ideas. The children have more vocabulary and language functions, including nouns, adjectives and adverbs, and they can tell us about their thoughts and feelings. They use language interactively. Their artwork is a representation of their cognitive and social developmental processes within their cultural, familial and school-based context. The collection of their artwork and stories helped us learn about how they understood internationalization and their place in the world.

In other early childhood settings around the world, documenting and analyzing children's art and stories is highly recommended because it can provide the school with data to make informed decisions about how to develop and internationalize the curriculum. No matter where a school is situated, and no matter what the culture or neighborhood, educators always have a lot to learn from the children. We improve and invent specific approaches to curriculum that are guided by our assessments of what the children are learning individually and in groups. Although spending time with children individually is not always possible for teachers, these kinds of sessions can take place with other adults, like volunteers, who can meet one to one with the children. It is worth the effort and the results may be informative and help the school and the teachers to further develop and adapt the global dimensions of their curriculum.

Method

The population of children were students in our school who were in the four-year-old classrooms. The majority of children had been through the internationalization process in their classrooms, and only a handful of children were new to the four-year-old group. They represented a cross section of the school's population, who came from different countries and from within the United States, and all were local residents. Some of the children had travelled to other countries and others had not. Because the children came from a variety of cultural backgrounds, they often spoke additional languages, and they were learning Spanish in our school. Children with special needs were included, with some children designated as having sensory integration disorders and some with speech and language delays and disorders.

The first set of data was collected at the conclusion of the first year of the internationalization process in our curriculum, and as the researcher, I initially tried to collect the children's drawings and stories in their actual classrooms. This was unsuccessful because of the numerous (and wonderful) educational distractions available in a busy classroom designed for four-year-olds. To help the children concentrate, the researcher decided to work with children individually in a separate room where the children would have my undivided attention and minimal auditory and visual distractions. White paper and a pencil were provided for each child in order to gain as much detail as possible. The children dictated their words to me, and I wrote what they said on another paper. Sometimes the children asked how to spell words and wrote those words on their own artwork, frequently looking at me for praise because they wanted me to see that they knew how to write letters. Occasionally the children asked me, as the researcher, to read back to them what they had dictated, and they enjoyed hearing their own words and ideas.

The sessions began with me providing a verbal prompt for the children to follow and respond to by drawing. At first it was, "Show me you as a citizen of the world". The majority of the children responded with confusion at the word "citizen", and so I had to explain and clarify by using other words. With an explanation, they were able to respond and interact by telling their stories and ideas. The children were comfortable with being in a room with me as the researcher because I had been a frequent visitor in their classrooms and they knew who I was. When they asked why I was doing this, I explained that I loved making art with children and listening to their words. Additionally, I gave them the option to conclude the sessions whenever they wanted, but almost all the children enjoyed private time and attention from an adult and they decided to stay and complete their artwork and dictated stories. They seemed happy and peaceful during their time with me as the researcher.

Following the second year of internationalizing our curriculum, the consolidation year, I had learned from an analysis of the research data that we were actually developing the foundations of children's global competence, not specifically their global citizenship. This was a major research finding and necessitated a change in the prompt for the collection of children's art and stories. I used the prompt, "Show me you making the world a better place." This prompt worked beautifully, with children responding and understanding the concept. They had also experienced two years of global knowledge infusion in their daily classroom lives, so they had more experience and could talk about what was happening in the world. Their responses varied along with their levels of cognitive development and their social-emotional awareness. Several children displayed genuine giftedness in their thinking, inventing solutions to the world's problems at four years of age, and suggesting social considerations, too, for example that everyone in the world should have a best friend.

A total of 70 children provided artwork and stories during the data collection process. The sample consisted of 32 children in the first year, from two classrooms of four-year-olds. In the second year, data was collected from 38 children in the four-year-old classrooms. The findings were basically conclusive but sometimes non-conclusive, as is often the case with an analysis of children's artwork and verbal productions. The research findings indicated that the children had learned a global perspective and they tried, with different levels of success, to merge local and global knowledge, which is evidence of their thought processes and the foundations of global competence. Their learned altruism emerged from the data, and many children readily took responsibility for others less fortunate and for the world's problems, showing their actual emerging global citizenship. The majority of the children were willing and eager to express their views about the world as they understood it. A more detailed analysis follows.

Research Findings

The children's artwork and stories were coded according to themes that emerged from the data, and were analyzed separately as Year One and Year Two. The themes in Year One represent the beginnings of our internationalization process of curriculum, and how the children were beginning to understand and make sense of their new dimension of knowledge.

The Year One primary and secondary themes were as follows:

1   *Content*

    a   Recycling and cleaning up trash
    b   Protecting natural environments and enjoying nature
    c   Taking care of each other and families and pets (altruism, kindness)
    d   Gift giving
    e   Solving problems and being a hero
    f   Combining locations to be "the world"
    g   Family themes considered to be "the world"

2   *Cognitive and Socio-Emotional Development*

    a   Process of drawing
    b   Cognitive combinations of the "world" and locations
    c   Self as able to accomplish things
    d   Visual images of the world

Content: Year One

The children were very concerned about caring for the earth and especially included pictures of themselves recycling and cleaning up messes, mostly outdoors. They identified and drew pictures of many items that had to be thrown away or recycled, for example, old bottles, strings, papers, cans, broken bottles, broken plates and ripped paper. Some drawings illustrated family members helping to clean up together. One child even drew a picture of an invention that he said was a robot who could clean up the ocean. Another child's artwork was about saving nature and she added schema of flowers, butterflies, clouds, sky, bees, rosebuds, monkeys, bears and zebras, naming each one distinctly. The children drew themselves as reusing things instead of throwing them away, too. Nature was frequently how they represented the world, but they often drew a circle to be the world, as a globe, and then visual images were added into their framework of the world. One child's artwork illustrated grass, dirt, flowers and sun, and she said that we have to care for nature by watering plants and trees. Taking care of animals was important and represented in several of the drawings and stories with dogs ("puppies"), bunnies and birds. Children wanted to feed and pet their cats and other animals in the world, and they drew and described domestic and wild animals without distinguishing between them.

A boy drew a shark who was aggressive and a dolphin who he needed to be saved from the shark. A different boy drew his friend and stated that we have to stop killing animals like lions, and that there should be no hitting either, so animals and friends would be safe.

Almost all the children expressed happiness about the world and the people in it. They exhibited caring and kindness in their drawings and stories. A little girl said that "it is happiness to be in the world". They spoke about Band-Aids and how we should take care of one another when we are hurt. Siblings getting along was part of the children's expressions in their artwork, and they illustrated their families as in the world, with one child including momma birds who should feed and care for their children. They drew images of gift giving in their homes and in the world, often extending the images outside of their houses. One child drew his nana and how she was feeding people in the world, in their family and all around. A girl wrote the words, "Love the world" on her picture, demonstrating her warm feelings of emotional connectedness and caring. A different child spoke about helping in cities and drew his schema of a city, with closed structures for buildings and he added some rudimentary versions of people in the city. Another child drew a series of presents as gifts to give to people that were toys, candy, a donut, and wrapped packages, almost reminiscent of a children's birthday party. A few children illustrated themselves as being heroes who would save the world from bad guys and included one boy stating, "I have to protect the world." Echoing this idea, another child drew himself as a superhero who had special powers and swords to "be strong and save others", as he emphatically stated. Another child specifically described and drew how he would build construction and do "hard work" because, he said, "I have to make stuff better."

Depictions of the world were somewhat uncertain and a range of attempts to define the world were obvious in the children's art and accompanying stories. They had the concept of "world" but expressed it differently. A few children seemed to have no idea about the concept of "world" and looked at the researcher with a blank expression on their faces. One of these children simply drew his family and immediate environment as the world. Another girl illustrated her family "sisters who are Mandarin" and her United States family, and she included Taiwan, as she told her story. For her, all those people represented the world. A different child actually drew the world as continents and countries, with different sections on his drawing for each concept, but he couldn't elaborate regarding what those words really meant. Confusion about location was frequently drawn as compartments on the drawings, and identified in many ways. One child said that "the United States is who lives in the world." A boy said that his drawing was of California, which in his mind was equivalent to the world. Defining the world as a sibling relationship, a girl said that her picture of herself and her sister was the "entire world". Another child drew an elaborate school bus situated in nature, and said that the bus was taking his family to the "whole world", which was the natural environment.

Cognitive and Socio-Emotional Development: Year One

The results of the actual drawing and storytelling process were not unexpected. There was a difference between children whose words were more advanced and complex than their images. Conversely, some children drew elaborate pictures but their dictated stories were minimal. Some children started work right away, while others spent time thinking first; others were purposeful and added meanings and details as they continued the process. A few children appeared to have special needs, with expressive or receptive language disorders and atypical cognitive processing, which made it difficult for them to understand my prompts as a researcher. One or two children sang songs while they made art, needing the auditory stimulation to accompany their visual expression. The majority of the children were able to focus their attention on the task and complete it, sometimes adding images and ideas. One or two of the children exhibited attentional problems and I had to continually refocus them on the task at hand. Some children needed a lot of verbal prompting, while others needed very little verbal direction. A few children seemed emotionally needy and enjoyed the one-on-one attention from an adult who was focused on their thoughts, feelings and creative expressions. One girl said, "I miss my mommy. She's at work. My heart and belly button are happy." There were a variety of different images, ranging from the simple to the complex, and representing children's development.

Cognitively, the children were struggling (in a positive way) to synthesize and combine ideas and figure out the interrelationships among people and locations. Their drawing reflected this cognitive challenge. For some children, the act of visually symbolically representing the world was transformative because they had to reflect upon their imagery after they made the picture. They learned from the process of thinking, drawing and telling their stories. An example of this attempt at understanding the world was a boy's drawing of the world that included mom, the water park, roller coasters, planets and the globe. The child drew himself at the center of the drawing, involved in all the activities. The world was represented as a big circle in most of the children's drawings, or at least a circle was included significantly somewhere on the page. Children included their homes and families as part of the world, and some images related to travel experiences. Several children were trying to determine the relationship of space travel and geography, in their own unique ways of thinking. When the world was drawn as a circle, the children varied in placing themselves inside and outside of the circle. In some instances the world or circle was bigger than the people, and for other children, the people were drawn as larger than the circle. For a few children, when the drawing process became a bit overwhelming, they drew stereotypic images like butterflies and hearts. One child seriously contemplated what Peru, China and the United States looked like and how they could be drawn. The result was some scribbles and some more refined visual schema. The placement on the page was awkward, depicting the child's attempt to understand and synthesize what the countries meant in terms of the whole world. Another child combined ideas to represent the world in his drawing as "trash mouse car". A few children gave human attributes to nature, like drawing a smiling sunshine and a happy tree, and repeatedly representing the world as nature and a garden. The majority of the children viewed themselves as capable to make the world a better place. Not one child doubted that possibility, and all the children felt able to accomplish things. They had strong schema for themselves, and the other people they drew were variations of their basic person schema, which began with themselves. Many children drew themselves as large, well placed on the page, and actively doing things in the world. Their attitudes and self-images were positive, and they were clearly aware of other people and the world around them.

At the end of Year Two, the children's drawings and stories were collected, representing a different group of children, most of whom had experienced two years of our internationalized curriculum. They had more experience with global ideas in the classroom, and with the international expansion of the classroom curriculum projects. The results of these findings showed increases in many areas of the children's understandings and view of the world. Although some of the themes were similar to the themes that emerged in year one, there were differences in the complexity of children's ideas and sense of agency.

The Year Two primary and secondary themes were:

1 *Content*

    a   Children's friendships and relationships
    b   Caring for the earth and love of nature
    c   Fantasy and personal life (media influences)
    d   Self as inventors, problem solvers and heroes
    e   Conceptualizing a schema of the world

2 *Cognitive and Socio-emotional Development*

    a   Process of drawing
    b   Self as problem solver, thinker and planner
    c   Distinguishing fantasy from reality, and memories
    d   Responsibility for others and understanding their perspectives

Content: Year Two

Four-year-olds typically experience the beginnings of friendships and are becoming increasingly able to recognize that other people have ideas that are different from their own. Socio-centricity as a stage of children's development was evident in the children's artwork and stories about how they would make the world a better place. Their vocabularies had increased and they were able to talk about their feelings. The children frequently drew pictures of their best friends and described them in their stories. They drew pictures of people holding hands, and images of sharing food together. They told personal narratives about friendships and in their artwork they differentiated the schema for people. Several children said that friends make the world a better place. One girl said that her friend had a birthday coming and that she and her friend were going to kindergarten with each other. Relationships were described by the children as ongoing, because they had an understanding of the future and could plan for and anticipate the continuation of friendships. Their worldviews were no longer only about themselves; they spoke about themselves living in a world of friendships and families. People were included in almost all their pictures.

Caring for the earth was depicted in more complex ways, with details of flowers, sunlight and seeds in the process of growing in the earth. One girl drew an apple tree so that everyone could eat and be strong in the world. Another child represented the world as "having eyes to see me and everywhere on earth". Some of the children were aware of global climate issues and a few actually drew pictures of the earth overheating and needing to be clean. One girl spoke of a garden with strawberries, mango trees, flowers and a rocket to the moon, indicating that there was more that she understood than her present immediate environment. Other children drew pictures of seeds and plants growing on the earth and they explained the sequence of how plants grow. One girl said, "I can draw a better world", and she proceeded to draw a nature scene with birds flying, the sun, flowers and apples.

Distinguishing fantasy from reality became a theme in the children's art and stories. Some children appeared to have been influenced by the media they have been exposed to, such as television and movies. Outer space travel and rocket ships were plentiful in the children's stories and pictures, and they spoke about space travel to get away from scary natural occurrences like volcanos and floods. Several of the children drew pictures from fantasy television shows. One child drew a picture about black holes and, although he couldn't explain what black holes were, he believed they were very scary. It was as though some of the children drew their fantasies and fears to somehow gain mastery over those emotions. A boy explained that if children ever lost their mom, they could go to another planet and get another mom. A little boy was very animated and excited as he drew rocket ships that blast off, and he told his story about other planets included that "they don't have humans there but they do have dangerous things." Stories of intergalactic travel, inspired by television, contained aspects of good and bad people, and the children wanted the good people to win. A girl made a picture of the sun lifting the children up because the sun wanted to meet them while the moon was sleeping. She attributed human characteristics to the sun and moon as a way of trying to make sense of the world beyond her neighborhood. A boy drew a picture of his family travelling overseas, and then he inserted a fantasy in the story by stating that he could get all his favorite animals there and bring them all home. He couldn't separate the fantasy from the reality of the family trip.

The children felt empowered to be inventors, problem solvers and heroes as they contemplated how they would make the world a better place. A girl said she would help poor people by giving them money and shoes in other countries, and she drew herself doing that. One of the children called himself an inventor and drew an invention of a machine to smooth out the snow so people can go skiing, and he also drew a house under the sea. His artwork contained many details of how undersea living would occur and how he was definitely going to invent that. Another child said he would build a robot to pick up garbage in the environment. A different child drew a picture of an ocean bird who would help him to clean up the trash in the ocean. In that case the bird was also the hero with the child. Confidently, a girl drew a self-portrait of herself being a police officer and said that she would "stop cars from going fast so they wouldn't make more smoke". She explained that in addition to being a police officer, she wanted to be a rock star, too, to make the world a better place. Another boy told me that he would save animals and that he wanted to save babies so they don't get hurt. His artwork showed him trying to accomplish those goals.

The children's conceptualizations of the "world" and "earth" were interconnected, and they sometimes used the words interchangeably. For one child, children playing, cleaning up and making a house defined the world. For another child, her family going camping represented the world. And another girl told me that the mermaid she drew swam all over the world and that the oceans and mermaids were the world. When the children considered the word "earth", they tended to draw pictures of the natural aspects of our planet, including pictures of land, clouds, water and volcanos, and sometimes they added buildings. One child's concept of the world was a trip she would take with her mother to pick up garbage and then return home. She drew two distinct places in her artwork, representing her awareness that the world consisted of different locations, however her idea was to go there with her mother, thereby taking someone dear and familiar with her.

Cognition and Socio-Emotional Development: Year Two

The children's process was similar to what transpired in year one, but this time the children exhibited more self-awareness and confidence. In response to my prompt, one boy smiled and said, "It's a good thing I know how to make humans." The children were able to somehow integrate their family life with global issues and knowledge. Some children need to draw and talk about their families first before they could address the global question. Because of their increased cognitive development and vocabulary, they were able to express their emotions and their capacity for reasoning. Often their stories were sequential, with beginnings and middles and endings. Most of the children knew when they were done with their art and stories, and informed me that it was "the end". The children seemed to watch me for my reactions, and they were surprised at my neutrality, no matter what they drew or expressed. As in Year One, there were a few children with special needs who couldn't participate because of thought processing and language disorders, so they couldn't understand what was being asked by my prompt as a researcher.

As mentioned previously, the children felt that they could solve problems and make an impact on the world. Some of the children could anticipate consequences and related to the world's problems, thinking about what might happen in the future. Many children had a future orientation and could see and think beyond their present environment. They were problem solvers and could connect ideas and situations, feeling that they were going to do important things in the world when they grow up. Their drawings and narratives expressed that sense of kindness and caring for others and for the world in concrete, practical ways. Due to increased exposure to international issues, they also began to reconfigure their inner understandings of what home is, and they tried to reconcile their four-year-old emotions with the scope of the world. For example, a boy explained his fear of the unknown, like space travel to other planets, and his corresponding fear that he might lose a parent. Conceptually the children were working hard to integrate places and circumstances other than their own, and this was reflected in their visual schema and stories. Their short and long term memories similarly had improved and they had learned that life happens with a past and a future, and that sense of placement in time applies to everywhere in the world, too. This was something their stories illustrated a level of confusion about, but the fact that they were even struggling to understand such abstract concepts was positive and heartening.

Media influences were definitely present in the children's conceptualizations about the world, and the children spoke and drew about media characters as if they existed in reality. It was challenging for the children to differentiate between reality and fantasy in the television and movie images they spoke and drew pictures of. Images such as mermaids, superheroes, princesses, space travel, strange lands and worlds, and indulgence in magical wish fulfillment seemed to be part of the thinking of several of the children. Some of the images were benign but some were scary, and it seemed that many of the children were watching negative and positive world news, and all sorts of shows, and that they definitely were sorting it out in their minds and incorporating what they viewed into their understanding of the world. To many of the children, the world was understood as divided into good and bad.

Learning from Children: How Would You Make the World a Better Place?

This chapter would not be complete without some notable quotes from the four-year-old children whose artwork and stories have been previously described. Teachers learn from and with young children every day, and they inspire and educate us without a doubt. I hope you will enjoy and reflect upon the children's words:

- I will hug everybody, make peace, hold hands and walk with each other. That's what peace means. They're holding hands and walking because they're all best friends. No dirty air. It's rain going to the flowers. All these things are in a peaceful world.
- The earth is kind of big, but Jupiter is bigger.
- Now I'm making my family and my family home. I want to make my world. I want to make my planet. Now I'm going to make my world a better place. All my family is here. Earth makes you wake up and sleep, and it's planet earth.
- OK. I'll draw it. No more oil spills. That's me, and this ship is sucking up all the oil from oil spills, for cars. It doesn't run on anything. It's a ship that floats over the sea. This is the pipe that sucks up the oil. If you have an oil spill, it will kill the fish and the fishermen won't catch fish to eat. It floats around the whole entire sea, in Africa and Asia and Florida and Hawaii and Antarctica. So the whole ocean has no more oil.
- By helping people, it makes me feel nice. By going all over the world and if we see someone that is poor or hurt, we can give them some Band-Aids or cream, and if they're very, very poor we can give them some shoes and we can also give them some money.
- This is a bank that has money, and people go there to get money, and if other people don't have money, they can get money and give some to them. I help to build the school, and I made the bike path with blocks like we have outside.
- The world has to have eyes to look at me and everywhere. The earth is so good, it is so healthy. The world sees me, and the world sees everybody. The world is what we do for peace and love. That's the world a better place. So kind.
- This is for people all around the world. It makes food. You press a button. It's for everyone and astronauts. I made the machine. I'm there. You press a button and it shoots out food in plastic bags. That's it. I invented.
- Picking up garbage all over. All the garbage gone so they're going inside so they can go to sleep. By cleaning up the garbage, it's the whole world.
- They're sharing toys so they can live and then everyone will be kind to each other. Being kind, no hitting, listen to each other and that's it.
- I'm on the earth. I am helping pick up garbage. I'm helping the robot. Done!
- Alright, now I've done my earth. I'm making water now. I did my whole earth, and this is the water, too. I made the world better because I put the water. First the people didn't have water to drink. And then I made water. The people were shouting "hoo-ray!" because they had water.
- They go in outer space. There's other planets. Maybe they're more. They don't have humans, but they have very dangerous things. That's me in the rocket ships. It's going to blast off, make it better.

- This is a net that's plastic. The fish thinks its food. The turtle's going to the plastic water bottle. This is a bird. She's going to help the sea animals not get sick from the garbage. She's going to get the veterinarian to help the fish get better.
- The world is right here. I'll carry it gently to the black hole to make it better. You put it inside the black hole and it takes it to a peaceful land, and the bad people get better and the good stay good. And the black hole takes it somewhere and they find another black hole to return to earth. The heart means love.
- To make the world a better place, to be an officer is to be a cop, and you can be a meter maid. I just learned it, and I think about it. They catch the bad guys, and then they put them in jail. I love being an officer and a rock star. I can be both of them. I love officers a lot!

Questions: What Did You Learn?

This chapter provided an analysis of the children's artwork and stories during the process of internationalizing our early childhood curriculum. The themes that emerged helped us to better understand how the children actually internalized and learned global knowledge and the foundations of global competence. If we are teaching children about the world, we benefit by collecting their ideas and imagery. In early childhood schools around the world, here are some questions to guide your analysis of the children's art and stories. These questions are just a beginning, and you will most likely add many more questions that relate to your own neighborhood, country and cultural context.

1. What are the basic themes that the children expressed in their artwork and stories?
2. How do the children conceptualize the "world" or "earth"?
3. How do the children incorporate their personal world of family and friends into their understanding of the world?
4. Do the children view themselves as capable and able to make the world a better place? Explain.
5. What do their drawings and stories reflect about their feelings and emotions about the world?
6. How do the children synthesize and/ or differentiate fantasy and reality in the ideas they express?
7. What did you learn about the influence of media on children's experience of the world?
8. What troubles children about the world? What did they express?
9. What delights children about the world? What did they express?
10. Did the children's responses reveal their relationship with nature and caring for the earth? If so, how?

11   How do the children understand the locations of different countries and regions beyond their immediate local environments?

12   How did the children express a sense of responsibility and caring for each other and for everyone in the world?

13   What did you, as their teacher, learn from the children's art and stories that can be applied to improving your internationalized early childhood curriculum in your classroom and school?

Summary

This chapter has provided a way for teachers to understand their own children's conceptualizations of the world, and their corresponding foundations of global competence. In a globally interconnected world, where knowledge is available and shared almost instantaneously throughout the world, our work as teachers is more important than ever before. Building on the prior chapters in this book, with a rationale for why we need to internationalize our curriculum, guidelines for the stages of internationalization, descriptions of classroom projects, and an analysis of teacher's transformations as global citizens, this chapter gives us a method for assessing what children are learning about the world, and how they comprehend their role in making the world a better place for all of humanity. The next and final chapter will offer an overview of the significance of this work for the profession of early childhood education.

6 Conclusions, Recommendations and Reflections

Introduction

The story of the internationalization of our early childhood curriculum has introduced you to the complexities, successes, challenges, learning and inspiration we experienced during the process. We offer our work to you as a beginning, a way to start thinking about how to bring global knowledge and an international perspective into your early childhood classrooms. Questions have been provided to help you move forward with your own curriculum expansion and change process. In every classroom, in every country, we all want what is best for our children, and our students' parents join us in hoping for a positive and productive future for the children. Recognizing that curriculum expectations vary across the world, and that access to knowledge about the world is uneven depending on economics, location, and access to technology, there may be many ways that children can learn about global knowledge and the foundations of global competence that haven't even been touched upon in this book. We encourage you to explore, to innovate and to make your curriculum internationalization process unique. All around the world we honor, celebrate and respect the children and their families, and the extraordinarily important role teachers and directors play in early childhood curriculum.

There are increasingly compelling reasons for consciously internationalizing curriculum because of the interconnectedness of knowledge and news being transmitted instantaneously from country to country. There are also growing global concerns for environmental issues in light of climate change, with the goal of sustainability. Global citizenship is, therefore, growing in importance from moment to moment, and the foundations of global competence in our youngest children are considered to be in the forefront of global educational reforms. This book consists of an introduction and six chapters that include a rationale for our work, guidelines for internationalization of early childhood curriculum, stories from our classrooms and professional development, transformational portraits of teachers, children's voices and artistic expressions and this final chapter about conclusions, reflections and new directions. Realistically, the identification of conclusions is an attempt to articulate a dynamic and constantly changing and expanding, and sometimes even contradictory and puzzling, learning process. What follows is an attempt to describe what we've learned so far.

Conclusions

1   Knowledge is global, even in everyday processes for young children. Ideas move from the local to the global; children's thinking happens simultaneously and in multiples. Children work to synthesize prior knowledge with increasing global information. Curriculum can transcend previously accepted limitations and expectations of what young children can learn. In the technological age, local knowledge may have already become global knowledge in some instances.

2   In early childhood curriculum, we are teaching children the *foundations of global competence, which leads to fully actualized global citizenship* in the future. Children's learning includes the interconnectedness of people and ideas, and their learning corresponds to their levels of cognitive and socio-emotional development. Children's alleged confused thinking is evidence that they are on the way to learning new concepts. They can learn through trial and error, multiple modalities, repetition and hands-on activities.

3   Local, national and global citizenship is not contradictory; rather, it is an expanded sense of identity to experience oneself as a citizen of a city and a nation, and also as belonging to the world. Children can understand that they are part of a big world and their immediate environment.

4   Teacher's lives transform dramatically by learning about the world and recognizing that they are also global citizens. Teachers learn at an adult level, while the children are learning at their own developmental pace. Parents who choose to get involved are learning to be global citizens in a broader sense as well. Time for self-reflection is helpful for teachers as their perspectives change. Teacher's play an essential role in helping children to develop the foundations of global competence.

5   Teacher's inner (usually visual) schemas of the world drive the internationalization of curriculum. Internal schemas of the world are inner constructs that are manifested from the inside out, in daily curriculum activities and interactions with children. It is valuable to explore teacher's inner schemas of the world, to help prevent any limiting perceptions of the world that might be transferred to young children through the curriculum. The Slattery teachers were asked to share their visual and conceptual schemas of the world, resulting in images that represented a) different countries and locations with a range of natural environments (beaches, mountains, and forests), b) wishes for a better world, c) global problems and d) autobiographical scenes from their lives. Teachers involved in internationalizing their curriculums should be made aware of their own

inner schema so they can reflect upon how what they believe about the world impacts on their classroom teaching. Attempts should be made to expand and extend teacher's inner schemas of the world through educational activities such as professional development.

6   The Sustainable Development Goals (SDGs) may contribute significantly to the core content of early childhood curriculum, preparing children to address goals agreed upon by the world community of nations. These goals should exist along with statewide and national learning standards for early childhood education. The SDGs can enhance curriculum and not replace what has already proved to be effective.

7   The director of the school plays a critically significant role in supporting the internationalization of early childhood curriculum by serving as an administrator and educator. The director's role is to encourage innovation and creative risk-taking, to mentor teachers on a regular basis, and to help identify and procure classroom resources. At Slattery, our director was an administrator and an educator, and was successful in negotiating both roles as she supported the teachers.

8   Internationalization of early childhood curriculum is situationally specific, however the stages of internationalization may have universal applicability. Schools need to follow or invent their curriculum change mechanisms, and assess progress continually.

9   Internationalization of curriculum in early childhood education may contribute to a new aspect of 21st century peace education, furthering Maria Montessori's original ideas about children's cultural learning about the countries of the world. In the technological age, global knowledge and its availability may add a new dimension to Maria Montessori's global curriculum formulations. The goal of establishing a culture of peace, which United Nations promotes, should be strongly emphasized. Education to promote a peaceful world strengthens all of humanity.

Recommendations

The range of philosophical, economic and cultural factors around the world makes the articulation of recommendations for the early childhood professional community problematic, therefore the following recommendations are offered and intended to stimulate thinking and creativity. The following recommendations are catalysts for implementation and discovery.

1   Schoolwide global activities are necessary to sustain and ensure the continuation of the internationalization process in the curriculum. In our school, the planning of an international garden with plants from around the world was a major innovation, sparked by the school's director. A global committee of teachers who meet regularly, and are supported by the director, would sustain the internationalization process, give ownership for the process to the teachers and support innovative schoolwide sharing

of curriculum ideas. Other schoolwide ideas might include the development of an international library of children's toys that parents and staff collect from around the world. Families could borrow these toys for their children to play with at home, and return them to the toy library at the due date. An actual library of international books for young children could be established, with books collected or donated from families or staff who travel abroad. This would enrich children's exposure to the world's children's stories from other countries. Special events in the school, such as an international schoolwide dinner, or an international art show in the school would enhance the international aspect of the curriculum and continuing learning for children, families and the teachers. The inclusion of grandparents' story-telling, if they are from different countries, would benefit everyone's increasing global knowledge.

2   Professional development is essential to help teachers begin thinking in new ways about the world and how they can bring the foundations of global competence into their classrooms. It begins with an exploration of how teachers identify themselves and their cultural backgrounds, and how they learn about the world. After they identify their sources of global knowledge, they are able to investigate otherwise previously unexplored sources of information about the world. Ideas, as well as very practical applications and opportunities for teachers to design to internationalize their curriculums, should be included. Professional development should address how the teachers can involve parents, and how they can embrace our local and global communities. Initially, an assessment of the teacher's global knowledge base should be made, and then a series of sequential adult learning activities should be planned and revised as the sessions continue. Observations in each classroom and feedback from the trainer are necessary to support global ideas being translated into developmentally appropriate learning activities for the children. The director is integral to the entire professional development series, so that a consistent and relevant approach is continued, and any concerns that arise can be shared and addressed. Successes and challenges need to be considered and included as part of professional development and shared learning among the teachers. Through professional development the value and meaning of global competence for young children should be emphasized, and teachers should be applauded for their important role in actualizing the internationalization of their early childhood curriculum.

3   Early childhood teacher education should expand to include an international dimension, in coursework, assignments, and theoretical knowledge that should not be dominated by the Western narrative. Global citizenship should be a goal for teachers. I am pleased that my department at the university offers a global education graduate course based on the Sustainable Development Goals. Other examples include a course I designed about play theory and practice which includes an

assignment about play around the world, where students do research and present about young children's toys and games in different countries. In the course on the creative arts in early childhood education, we address cultural art artifacts from different countries and how they can be developed into art activities for young children, like silk batik from Malaysia and fabric collages from Columbia. In the undergraduate curriculum course, we discuss how young children understand the global news they hear on television, and how we can help them deal with their emotions, for example, when they hear about a volcano or tsunami. In a graduate course, we examine different early childhood curriculum models and standards from the different Ministries of Education around the world. Several of my doctoral students are conducting their research in different countries to gain a broad understanding of issues from a global perspective. We also study the United Nations Convention on the Rights of the Child and the country reports. Authentic conceptualizations of countries should be promoted by direct interviews with people who live or have lived in those countries, and not information gained through secondary sources alone. Every attempt should be made to internationalize the early childhood teacher education curriculum.

4 Research from different countries and regions about their own processes of internationalizing the early childhood curriculum is needed, to provide a greater perspective and to significantly increase our understanding of what it means to develop the foundations of global competence in young children, and global citizenship in teachers. Early childhood settings in public schools, private schools, faith based schools, non-governmental organization sponsored schools, corporate preschools and day care centers should internationalize their curriculums and conduct research about what transpires. In that way, we can gain a wide lens on what global competence means around the world and how children and their teachers and parents experience internationalized curriculum. Research provides us with a view of the world we might not otherwise experience, and we can learn from each other. Additionally, university demonstration lab schools around the world, and community-based model programs can serve as global research sites. It is imperative, however, that no one way is perceived or promoted as the best way to internationalize. There are as many ways to do this as there are early childhood schools in the world.

Reflections

I never anticipated writing the final paragraph of this book, and, in all honesty, I'm humbly at the beginning of the journey. The teachers who have read this book are now aware of my passionate dedication to early childhood education. We are a network of early childhood educators in every city and country who wake up every morning, go into our classrooms, and give our best to the children we teach. Teachers are proud, professional and caring people. During the years I've worked at the Slattery School, I have been profoundly moved by the teachers, children, parents and director. Their generosity of heart and commitment to the children has been exemplary and inspiring. It seems like the core of the internationalization process is about how we can hold in our minds many realities in the world that go on simultaneously. The more we can stretch our minds to include other realities and countries and places in the world where children live and learn, the better we can share global competence and global citizenship with them. How we can contain multiple realities is a question that certainly requires further investigation and discovery. The capacity to understand each other across borders is the cornerstone of early childhood peace education. I am still haunted by the words of the boy I mentioned at the beginning of this book who asked why we have war. On behalf of all children everywhere, my deepest wish is that through international understanding we can do better and create together a peaceful world. We live in the information age and the world has significantly changed. Knowledge is abundant and available on the internet and so creativity, innovation and communication are increasingly important in education now and in the future. What we need is the internationalization of early childhood curriculum and a pedagogy of profound love. It has been my great privilege and honor to share this work with you.

Bibliography

Acedo, C., & Hughes, C. (2014). Principles for learning and competences in the 21st-century curriculum. *Prospects*, 44(4), 503–525.

Acevedo, M. V. (2016). Classroom contexts that support young children's intercultural understanding. *Young Children*, 71(3), 37–42.

Anderson, R., & Braud, W. (2011). *Transforming self and others through research: Transpersonal research methods and skills for the human sciences and humanities*. Albany: State University of New York.

Ardalan, G. (2017). Spreading happiness: A preschool classroom in Washington, DC, investigates citizenship and makes a statement—"Be Happy!" *Young Children*, 72(2), 64–71.

Asia Society (2010). *Ready for the world: Preparing elementary students for the global age*. New York: Asia Society.

Association for Childhood Education International (1999). *Early childhood education and care in the 21st century*. Ruschikon: ACEI & OMEP.

Azzam, A. M. (2014). Motivated to learn: A conversation with Daniel Pink. *Educational Leadership*, 72(1), 12–17.

Ban, K-M. (2012a, September). *An initiative of the secretary-general: Statement from the secretary-general*. Retrieved from www.unesco.org/new/en/gefi/about/an-initia tive-of-the-sg/

Ban, K-M. (2012b, September). *Global education first initiative: The UN Secretary-General's global initiative: Priority #3: Foster global citizenship*. Retrieved from www.unesco.org/new/en/gefi/priorities/global-citizenship

Banks, J. A. (2016). *Cultural diversity and education: Foundations, curriculum, and teaching*. New York: Routledge.

Barbour, N., & McBride, B. A. (2017). *The future of child development lab schools: Applied developmental science in action*. New York: Routledge.

Barnes, M. (2015). *5 Skills for the global learner: What everyone needs to navigate the digital world*. Thousand Oaks, CA: Corwin Press.

Batelle for Kids. (2019). *Partnership for 21st century learning: A network of Batelle for Kids*. Retrieved from www.battelleforkids.org/networks/p21/frameworks-resources

Belafonte, H., & Rayner, A. (Eds.) (2002). *A life like mine: How children live around the world*. New York: Dorling Kindersley in association with UNICEF.

Bell, D., Jean-Sigur, R. E., & Kim, Y. A. (2015). Going global in early childhood education. *Childhood Education*, 91(2), 90–91.

Bennett, L. B., Aguayo, R. C., & Field, S. L. (2016). At home in the world: Supporting children in human rights, global citizenship, and digital citizenship. *Childhood Education*, 92(3), 189–199.

Bergen, D., & Hardin, B. (2013). Cross-cultural collaboration research to improve early childhood education. In S. Wortham (Ed.), *Common characteristics and unique qualities in preschool programs: Global perspectives in early childhood education* (pp.13–20). New York: Springer.

Bjorklund, D.(2012). *Children's thinking: Cognitive development and individual differences*(3rd ed.). Belmont, CA: Wadsworth, Cengage Learning.

Bloch, M., Kennedy, D., Lightfoot, T., & Weyenberg, D. (Eds.) (2006). *The child in the world/the world in the child: Education and the configuration of a universal, modern, and globalized childhood*. New York: Palgrave Macmillan.

Brody, D. L. (2014). *Men who teach young children: An international perspective*. London: Trentham.

Brown, S. C., & Kysilka, M. L. (2009). *Multicultural and global education: What every teacher should know about multicultural and global education*. Boston, MA: Pearson.

Brunold-Conesa, C. (2011). International education: The international baccalaureate, Montessori and global citizenship. *Journal of Research in International Education*, 9(3), 259–272.

Care, E., Kim, H., Anderson, K., & Gustafsson-Wright, E. (2017, April). *Skills for a changing world: National perspectives and the global movement*. Retrieved from https://www.brookings.edu/wp-content/uploads/2017/03/global-20170324-skills-for-a-changing-world.pdf

Carroll, K. (2015). Going global. In R. Reynolds, D. Bradbery, J. Brown, K. Carroll, D. Donnelly, K. Ferguson-Patrick, & S. Macqueen (Eds.), *Contesting and constructing international perspectives in global education* (pp.151–158). Rotterdam: Sense Publishers.

Chan, L. K. S., & Mellor, E. J. (2002). *International developments in early childhood services*. New York: Peter Lang.

Church, E. B. (2016). *Nurturing next-generation innovators: Open-ended activities to support global thinking*. Lewisville, NC: Gryphon House.

Collins, M. (2008). *Global citizenship for young children*. Thousand Oaks, CA: SAGE.

Cookson, P. W. (2009). What would Socrates say? *Educational Leadership*, 67(1), 8–14.

Copple, C. (2011). *A world of difference: Readings on teaching young children in a diverse society*. Washington, DC: National Association for the Education of Young Children.

Copple, C., & Bredekamp, S. (2009). *Developmentally appropriate practice in early childhood programs: Serving children from birth through age 8*. Washington, DC: NAEYC.

Costa, A., & Kallick, B. (2010). It takes some getting used to: Rethinking curriculum for the 21st century. In H. Hayes Jacobs (Ed.), *Curriculum 21: Essential Education for a Changing World* (pp.210–226). Alexandria, VA: ASCD.

Cuffaro, H. K. (1995). *Experimenting with the world: John Dewey and the early childhood classroom*. New York: Teachers College Press.

Cutler, K., Bersani, C., Hutchins, P., Bowne, M., Lash, M., Kroeger, J., Brokmeier, S., Venhuizien, L., & Black, F. (2012). Laboratory schools as places of inquiry: A collaborative journey for two laboratory schools. *Early Education and Development*, 23(2), 242–258.

Dahlberg, G., Moss, P., & Pence, A. (1999). *Beyond quality in early childhood education and care: Postmodern perspectives* (2nd ed.). Philadelphia, PA: Falmer Press, Taylor and Francis, Inc.

Davy, I. (2011). Learners without borders: A curriculum for global citizenship. *International Baccalaureate Organization*, 1–10.

Derman-Sparks, L.LeeKeenan, D., & Nimmo, J. (2015). *Leading anti-bias early childhood programs: A guide for change*. New York: Teachers College Press and NAEYC.

Donohue, C.(Ed.) (2015). *Technology and digital media in the early years: Tools for teaching and learning*. New York and Washington, DC: Routledge Press and NAEYC.

Douglass, A. L. (2017). *Leading for change in early care and education: Cultivating leadership from within*. New York: Teachers College Press.

Duckworth, C. (2006). Teaching peace: A dialogue on the Montessori method. *Journal of Peace Education*, 3(1), 39–53.

Duncan, A. (2011). Statement on International Education Week 2011. Retrieved from https://ed.gov/about/inits/ed/internationaled/2011-iew.html

Early Childhood Peace Consortium (2013, November 18). *The global launch event*. Retrieved from www.unicef.org/earlychildhood/index_70959.html

Ebbeck, M. (2006). The challenges of global citizenship. Some issues for policy and practice in early childhood education. *Childhood Education*, 82(6), 353–357.

Elicker, J., & Barbour, N. (2012). Introduction to the special issue on university laboratory preschools in the 21st century. *Early Education and Development*, 23(2), 139–142.

Engdahl, I. (2015). Early childhood education for sustainability: The OMEP world project. *International Journal of Early Childhood*, 47(3), 347–366.

File, N. (2012). Identifying and addressing challenges to research in university laboratory preschools. *Early Education and Development*, 23(2), 143–152. doi:10.1080/10409289.2012.619136.

File, N., Mueller, J. J., & Wisneski, D. B. (2012). *Curriculum in early childhood education: Re- examined, rediscovered, renewed*. New York: Routledge.

File, N., Mueller, J. J., Wisneski, D. B., & Stremmel, A. J. (2017). *Understanding research in early childhood education: Quantitative and qualitative methods*. New York: Routledge.

Gaudelli, W. (2003). *World class: Teaching and learning in global times*. Mahwah, NJ: Lawrence Erlbaum Associates Publishers.

Gaudelli, W. (2016). *Global citizenship education: Everyday transcendence*. New York: Routledge.

Geist, E. (2016). Let's make a map: The developmental stages of children's map-making. *Young Children*, 71(2), 50–55.

Genishi, C., & Goodwin, A. L. (Eds.) (2009). *Diversities in early childhood education: Rethinking and doing*. New York: Routledge.

Gerzon, M. (2005). *Leading beyond borders: A handbook for global citizens*. n.p.: Mark Gerzon.

Gerzon, M. (2010). *American citizen, global citizen: How expanding our identities makes us safer, stronger, wiser-and builds a better world*. Boulder, CO: SpiritScope Publisher.

Goffin, S. G. (2013). *Early childhood education for a new era: Leading for our profession*. New York: Teacher College Press.

Gonzalez-Mena, J. (2008). *Diversity in early care and education*. Boston, MA: McGraw-Hill.

Grieshaber, S., & Cannella, G. S. (Eds.) (2001). *Embracing identities in early childhood education: Diversity and possibilities.* New York: Teachers College Press.

Hancock, R. E. (2017). A world called home: Global citizenship education at sunshine preschool. *Childhood Education*, 93(6), 466–474.

Hancock, R. E. (2017). Global citizenship education: Emancipatory practice in a New York preschool. *Journal of Research in Childhood Education*, 31(4), 571–580.

Hansen, D. T. (2011). *The teacher and the world: A study of cosmopolitanism as education.* New York: Routledge.

Harris, P., & Manatakis, H. (2013). *Children as citizens: Engaging with the child's voice in educational settings.* New York: Routledge.

Hartman, S. (2017). Rurally located teacher candidates: Globalizing the early childhood social studies curriculum. *Dimensions of Early Childhood*, 45(3), 11–16.

Hayes Jacobs, H. (Ed.) (2010). *Curriculum 21: Essential education for a changing world.* Alexandria, VA: ASCD.

Herrera, S. G. (2010). *Biography-driven culturally responsive teaching.* New York: Teachers College Press.

Hobson, D. P., & Silova, I. (Eds.) (2014). *Globalizing minds: Rhetoric and realities in international schools.* Charlotte, NC: Information Age Publishing, Inc.

Hoot, J. L., Bakuza, F. R., Lavasani, M. G., Park, S. R., Sharifan, M. S., & Szecsi, T. (2016). Globalization: International perspectives on early childhood teacher education. In L. J. Couse & S. L. Recchia (Eds.), *Handbook of early childhood teacher education* (pp.348–363). New York: Routledge.

Huaman, E. S., & Brayboy, B. M. J. (Eds.) (2017). *Indigenous innovations in higher education: Local knowledge and critical research.* Rotterdam: Sense Publishers.

Huggins, V. (2013). Widening awareness of international approaches: An imperative for twenty-first-century early years practitioners? In J. Georgeson & J. Payler (Eds.), *International perspectives on early childhood education and care* (pp.9–17). Maidenhead: Open University Press.

International Affairs Office (n.d.). *Global and cultural competency.* Retrieved from https://sites.ed.gov/international/global-and-cultural-competency/

International Baccalaureate (2014). *The IB Primary Years Programme: The written curriculum.* Retrieved from www.ibo.org/programmes/primary-years-programme/curriculum/written-curriculum/

International Education Advisory Board (n.d.). *Learning in the 21st century: Teaching today's students on their terms.* Retrieved from www.certiport.com/Portal/Common/DocumentLibrary/IEAB_Whitepaper040808.pdf

International Step by Step Association (2010). *Competent educators of the 21st century: Principles of quality pedagogy.* Retrieved from www.issa.nl/sites/default/files/pdf/Publications/quality/Quality-Princioles-final-WEB.pdf

International Step by Step Association (2012). *Competent educators of the 21st century: Principles of quality pedagogy.* Retrieved from file:///C:/Users/Y/Downloads/ISSA%20Quality-Principles%20ENGLISH%20(1).pdf

Ionescu, M., & Tankersley, D. (2016). The ISSA principles of quality pedagogy: Quality early childhood education and care through democratic processes. *Learning for Wellbeing Magazine*, (1), 1–8.

Israel, R. (2012). *Global citizenship: A path to building identity and community in a globalized world.* Lexington, KY: CreateSpace Independent Publishing Platform.

Jackson, A. (2016). The antidote to extremism. *Educational Leadership*, 74(4), 18–23.

Jacobs, H. H. (Ed.) (2010). *Curriculum 21: Essential education for a changing world.* Alexandria, VA: ASCD.

Jacobs, H. H. (Ed.) (2014). *Mastering global literacy: Contemporary perspectives on literacy.* Bloomington, IN: Solution Tree Press.

Jean-Sigur, R., Bell, D., & Kim, Y. (2016). Building global awareness in early childhood teacher preparation programs. *Childhood Education, 92*(1), 3–9.

Kennedy, A. S., & Heineke, A. (2014). Re-envisioning the role of universities in early childhood teacher preparation: Partnerships for 21st century learning. *Journal of Early Childhood Teacher Education, 35*(3), 226–243.

Kindersley, B., & Kindersley, A. (1995). *Children just like me: A unique celebration of children around the world.* New York: Dorling Kindersley in association with UNICEF.

Kirkwood, D., Shulsky, D., & Willis, J. (2014). Beyond piñatas, fortune cookies, and wooden shoes: Using the world wide web to help children explore the whole wide world. *Childhood Education, 90*(1), 11–19.

Klein, J. D. (2017). *The global education guidebook: Humanizing K-12 classrooms worldwide through equitable partnerships.* Bloomington, IN: Solution Tree Press.

Lappalainen, R. (2018). Bridge 47: Building global citizenship. *Childhood Education, 94*(3), 41–44.

Larter, S. (Ed.) (2016). *Children just like me: A new celebration of children around the world.* New York: Dorling Kindersley Publisher.

Lasonen, J., & Teräs, M. (2016). Teachers' intercultural competence as part of global competence. In A. G. Welch & S. Areepattamannil (Eds.), *Dispositions in Teacher Education* (pp.221–233). Rotterdam: Sense Publishers.

Lea, K. (2011, January 23). *It's good to get global! Global citizenship in the early years.* Retrieved from https://eyfs.info/articles.html/general/its-good-to-get-global-global-citizenship-in-the-early-years-r69/

Leckman, J. F., Panter-Brick, C., & Salah, R. (Eds.) (2014). *Pathways to peace: The transformative power of children and families.* Cambridge, MA: The MIT Press.

Lee, I., & Yelland, N. (2014). The global childhood project: Complexities of learning and living with a bi-literate and trilingual literacy policy. In M. N. Bloch, B. B. Swadener, & G. S. Cannella (Eds.), *Reconceptualizing early childhood care & education: A reader: Critical questions, new imaginaries and social activism* (pp.313–324). New York: Peter Lang.

Levine, P. (2016). The question each citizen must ask. *Educational Leadership, 73*(6), 30–34.

Louis, S. (2009). *Knowledge and understanding of the world in the early years foundation stage.* New York: Routledge.

Loveless, D., Beverly, C. L., Bodle, A., Dredger, K. S., Foucar-Szocki, D., Harris, T., Kang, S. J., & Wishon, P. (2016). *The vulnerability of teaching and learning in a selfie society.* Rotterdam: Sense Publishers.

Martin, J. C. (2016). *Give your child the world: Raising globally minded kids one book at a time.* Grand Rapids, MI: Zondervan.

Mauro, L. (2017, June 17). *Connecting to the global goals through experiential learning.* Retrieved from www.teachsdgs.org/blog/connecting-to-the-global-goals-through-experiential-learning

McBride, B. A., Groves, M., Barbour, N., Horm, D., Stremmel, A., Lash, M., & Toussaint, S. (2012). Child development laboratory schools as generators of knowledge in early childhood education: New models and approaches. *Early Education & Development, 23*(2), 153–164.

Meier, D. R. (2014). International early childhood education: Unsettled issues, new possibilities. In L. R. Kroll & D. R. Meier (Eds.), *Educational change in international early childhood contexts: Crossing borders of reflection* (pp.21–35). New York: Routledge.

Mindes, G. (2014). *Social studies for young children: Preschool and primary curriculum anchor* (2nd ed.). Lanham, MD: Rowman & Littlefield Education.

Mindes, G. (2015). Preschool through grade 3: Pushing up the social studies from early childhood education to the world. *Young Children*, 70(3), 10–15.

Moss, P. (2014). *Transformative change and real utopias in early childhood education: A story of democracy, experimentation and potentiality.* New York: Routledge.

Mueller, J. J., & File, N. K. (2015). Teacher preparation in changing times: One program's journey toward re-vision and revision. *Journal of Early Childhood Teacher Education*, 36(2), 175–192.

Murphy, E. (Ed.) (2011). *Welcoming linguistic diversity in early childhood classrooms: Learning from international schools.* Buffalo, NY: Multilingual Matters.

Murphy, Y. (2017). Interdependence toward humaneness. *Childhood Education*, 93(3), 263.

Myers, R. (1995). *The twelve who survive: Strengthening programmes of early childhood development in the Third World* (2nd ed.). Ypsilanti, MI: High/Scope Press.

National Council for the Social Studies (2002). *National curriculum standards for social studies: A framework for teaching, learning and assessment.* Silver Springs, MD: National Council for the Social Studies.

National Council for the Social Studies (2013). *Revitalizing civic learning in our schools: A position statement of national council for the social studies.* Retrieved from www.socialstudies.org/positions/revitalizing_civic_learning

National Council for the Social Studies (2014). *National curriculum standards for social studies: executive summary.* Retrieved from www.socialstudies.org/standards/execsummary.

National Council for the Social Studies (2016). *Global and international education in social studies.* Retrieved from www.socialstudies.org/positions/global_and_international_education

National Council for the Social Studies (n.d.). *National curriculum standards for social studies: Executive summary.* Retrieved from www.socialstudies.org/standards/execsummary

Noddings, N. (2012). *Philosophy of education* (3rd ed.). Boulder, CO: Westview Press.

Noe, L. R. (2014). Internationalizing your early childhood college program. *Young Children*, 69(5), 58–65.

Noe, L. R. (2017). Returning home from international experiences: My new understanding of developmentally appropriate practices. *Young Children*, 72(4), 43–48.

Odhiambo, E. A., Chrisman, J. K., & Nelson, L. (2016). *Social studies and young children.* Boston, MA: Pearson.

O'Neill, C., & Brinkerhoff, M. (2018). *Five elements of collective leadership for early childhood professionals.* St. Paul, MN: Redleaf Press.

Paquette, K. (2009). *Pathways to peace: Lessons to inspire peace in the early childhood classroom.* Bloomington, IN: iUniverse.

Park, E., & Wagner, J. T. (2017). OMEP-Policy Forum: A call to action: Early childhood education on the global agenda at last. *International Journal of Early Childhood*, 49(3), 429–432.

Parnell, W., & Lorio, J. M. (Eds.) (2015). *Disrupting early childhood education research: Imagining new possibilities*. New York: Routledge.

Penn, H. (2011). *Quality in early childhood services: An international perspective*. New York: Open University Press.

Perkins, D. N. (2014). *Future wise: Educating our children for a changing world*. San Francisco, CA: Jossey-Bass.

Piirto, J. (2011). *Creativity for 21st century skills: How to embed creativity into the curriculum*. Rotterdam: Sense Publishers.

Pink, D. H. (2006). *Whole new mind: Why right-brains will rule the future*. New York: Penguin Group.

Pohan, C. A. (2003). Creating caring and democratic communities in our classrooms and schools. *Childhood Education, 79*(6), 369–373.

Pota, V. (2017). The future of education: Innovations needed to meet the sustainable development goals. *Child Education, 93*(5), 368–371.

Powell, W., & Kusuma-Powell, O. (2011). *How to teach now: Five keys to personalized learning in the global classroom*. Alexandria, VA: ASCD Publications.

P21's Framework for State Action on Global Education (n.d.). *Framework for state action on global education*. Retrieved from www.p21.org/storage/documents/Global_Education/P21_State_Framework_on_Global_Education_New_Logo.pdf

Puerling, B. (2012). *Teaching in the digital age: Smart tools for age 3 to grade 3*. St. Paul, MN: Redleaf Press.

Ramsey, P. G. (2015). *Teaching and learning in a diverse world: Multicultural education for young children* (4th ed.). New York: Teachers College.

Rapoport, A. (2015). Global citizenship education: Classroom teachers' perspectives and approaches. In J. Harshman, T. Augustine, & M. M. Merryfield (Eds.), *Research in global citizenship education* (pp.119–135). Charlotte, NC: Information Age Publishing.

Reardon, B. (Ed.) (1988). *Educating for global responsibility: Teacher-designed curricula for peace education, K-12*. New York: Teachers College Press.

Reimers, F. M. (2016). *Wrapping our minds around the world: Countries must teach their students to be stewards of inclusive and sustainable development*. Retrieved from www.usnews.com/news/best-countries/articles/2016-08-12/education-must-focus-on-globalization

Reimers, F. M. (2017). *One student at a time: Leading the global education movement*. North Charleston, SC: CreateSpace Independent Publishing Platform.

Reimers, F. (2018, May 2). *From a nation at risk to a democracy at risk: Educating students for democratic renewal*. Retrieved from www.brookings.edu/blog/education-plus-development/2018/05/02/from-a-nation-at-risk-to-a-democracy-at-risk-educating-students-for-democratic-renewal/

Reimers, F. M., Chopra, V., Chung, C. K., Higdon, J., & O'Donnell, E. B. (2016). *Empowering global citizens: A world course*. North Charleston, SC: CreateSpace Independent Publishing Platform.

Reimers, F. M., & Chung, C. K. (2016). *Teaching and learning for the twenty-first century: Educational goals, policies, and curricula from six nations*. Cambridge, MA: Harvard Education Press.

Reimers, F. M., et al. (2017). *Empowering students to improve the world in sixty lessons*. North Charleston, SC: CreateSpace Independent Publishing Platform.

Richey, A., & Her, L. (2016). Contesting institutional epistemologies of diversity: The shift to a global/ local framework in teacher education. In L. Nganga & J.

Kambutu (Eds.), *Social justice education, globalization, and teacher education* (pp.53–70). Charlotte, NC: Information Age Publishing.

Robles de Melendez, W., Beck, V., & Fletcher, M. (2000). *Teaching social studies in early education*. Belmont, CA: Delmar Thomson Learning.

Rosebrough, T. R., & Leverett, R. G. (2011). *Transformational teaching in the information age: making why and how we teach relevant to students*. Alexandria, VA: ASCD.

Samuelsson, I. P., & Park, E. (2017). How to educate children for sustainable learning and for a sustainable world. *International Journal of Early Childhood*, 49(3), 273–285.

Santone, S. (2019). *Reframing the curriculum: Design for social justice and sustainability*. New York: Routledge.

Seefeldt, C., Castle, S., & Falconer, R. C. (2010). *Social studies for the preschool/primary child* (8th ed.). Upper Saddle River, NJ: Pearson.

Seldin, T. (2010). Montessori and the international baccalaureate. *Tomorrow's Child*, 18(4), 5–9.

Selig, G., Arroyo, A., Jordan, H., Baggaley, K., & Hunter, E. (2010). *Loving our differences for teachers*. Boston, MA: Pearson Learning Solutions.

Sellers, M. (2013). *Young children becoming curriculum: Deleuze, Te Whāriki and curricular understandings*. New York: Routledge.

Shirley, D. (2016). *The new imperatives for educational change: Achievement with integrity*. New York: Routledge.

Short, K. G., Day, D., & Schroeder, J. (Eds.) (2016). *Teaching globally: Reading the world through literature*. Portland, ME: Stenhouse publishers.

Sledd, M. (2015, April 2). *The 8 skills students must have for the future*. Retrieved from www.edudemic.com/new-skills-world-looking/

Smidt, S. (2013). *The developing child in the 21st century: A global perspective on child development* (2nd ed.). New York: Routledge.

Sole, J. (2015, May). *10 hallmarks of 21st century teaching and learning*. Retrieved from www.edutopia.org/discussion/10-hallmarks-21st-century-teaching-and-learning

Souto-Manning, M. (2013). *Multicultural teaching in the early childhood classroom: Approaches, strategies and tools, preschool-2nd grade*. New York: Teachers College Press.

Souto-Manning, M. (2017). Generative text sets: Tools for negotiating critically inclusive early childhood teacher education pedagogical practices. *Journal of Early Childhood Teacher Education*, 38(1), 79–101.

Souto-Manning, M., Madrigal, R., Malik, K., & Martell, J. (2016). Bridging languages, cultures, and worlds through culturally relevant leadership. In S. Long, M. Souto-Manning, & V. M. Vasquez (Eds.), *Courageous leadership in early childhood education: Taking a stand for social justice* (pp.57–68). New York: Teachers College Press.

Spring, J. H. (Ed.) (2015). *Globalization of education: An introduction* (2nd ed.). New York: Routledge.

Stephenson, S. M. (2013). *Child of the world: Montessori, global education for age 3–12+*. Arcata, CA: Michael Olaf Montessori Company.

Stephenson, S. M. (2013). *The joyful child: Montessori, global wisdom for birth to three* (2nd ed.). Arcata, CA: Michael Olaf Montessori Company.

Strickland, T., & DePalma, K. (2016). *The barefoot book of children*. Bath: Barefoot Books.

Swiniarski, L. B., & Breitborde, Mary-Lou. (2003). *Educating the global village: Including the young child in the world* (2nd ed.). Upper Saddle River, NJ: Merrill/Prentice Hall.

Tanner, L. (1997). *Dewey's laboratory school: Lessons for today.* New York: Teacher's College Press.

Tavangar, H. S. (2009). *Growing up global: Raising children to be at home in the world.* New York: Ballantine Books.

Thomas, D., & Brown, J. S. (2011). *A new culture of learning: Cultivating the imagination for a world of constant change.* North Charleston, SC: CreateSpace Independent Publishing Platform.

Tichnor-Wagner, A. (2017). Inspiring glocal citizens. *Educational Leadership, 75*(3), 69–73.

Torres, V., Howard-Hamilton, M. F., & Cooper, D. L. (2003). *Identity development of diverse populations: Implications for teaching and administration in higher education: ASHE-ERIC higher education report.* San Francisco, CA: Jossey-Bass.

Trilling, B., & Fadel, C. (2012). *21st century skills: Learning for life in our times.* San Francisco, CA: Jossey-Bass.

Twum-Danso Imoh, A., & Ame, R. (2012). *Childhoods at the intersection of the local and the global.* New York: Palgrave Macmillan.

UNESCO (2014). *Global citizenship education: Preparing learners for the challenges of the 21st Century.* Paris: UNESCO.

UNESCO (2016). *Schools in action: Global citizens for sustainable development: A guide for students.* Retrieved from http://unesdoc.unesco.org/images/0024/002463/246352e.pdf

UNESCO (2016). *Schools in action: Global citizens for sustainable development: A guide for teachers.* Retrieved from http://unesdoc.unesco.org/images/0024/002463/246352e.pdf

UNICEF (2013, November 18). *Early childhood peace consortium.* Retrieved from www.unicef.org/earlychildhood/files/Early_Childhood_Peace_Consortium_Concept_Note_09_13_2013.pdf

UNICEF (2014). *The state of the world's children 2015: Reimagine the future: Innovation for every child.* New York: UNICEF.

UNICEF (2017, April 21). *Peace building through early childhood development: A guidance note.* Retrieved from www.saferspaces.org.za/uploads/files/UNICEF_ECD_and_peacebuilding.pdf

UNICEF (2017). *The state of the world's children 2017: Children in a digital world.* New York: UNICEF.

UNICEF (2017). *Learning for peace: Advancing learning. Building peace.* New York: UNICEF.

UNICEF (2018). *UNICEF Annual Report 2017.* New York: UNICEF.

United States Department of Education (2012, November). *Succeeding globally through international education and engagement: U.S. Department of Education international strategy 2012–2016.* Retrieved from www.actfl.org/sites/default/files/reports/international-strategy-2012-16.pdf

Verma, R.(2017). *Critical peace education and global citizenship: Narratives from the unofficial curriculum.* New York: Routledge.

Villareale, C. (2009). *Learning from the children: Reflecting on teaching.* St. Paul, MN: Redleaf Press.

Wagner, T. (2010). *The global achievement gap: Why even our best schools don't teach the new survival skills our children need – and what we can do about it.* New York: Basic Books.

Walker, G.(2010). *Challenges from a new world.* Melton: John Catt Educational.

Wallace, M. (2006). *Social studies: All day every day in the early childhood classroom*. Belmont, CA: Delmar Cengage Learning.

Westheimer, J. (2015). *What kind of citizen? Educating our children for the common good*. New York, NY: Teachers College Press.

Williams, R. D., & Lee, A. (Eds.) (2015). *Internationalizing higher education: Critical collaborations across the curriculum*. Rotterdam: Sense Publishers.

Woodrow, C., & Press, F. (2007). (Re)Positioning the child in the policy/politics of early childhood. *Educational Philosophy and Theory*, 39(3), 223–236.

Woodrow, C., & Press, F. (2008). (Re)Positioning the child in the policy/politics of early childhood. In S. Farquhar & P. Fitzsimons (Eds.), *Philosophy of early childhood education: Transforming narratives* (pp.88–101). Malden, MA: Blackwell Publishing.

Wortham, S. C. (2001). Global guidelines for the education and care of young children: The work continues. *Childhood Education*, 78(1), 42–43.

York, S. (2003). *Roots and wings: Affirming culture and preventing bias in early childhood*. St. Paul, MN: Redleaf Press.

Zeichner, K. (2009). Rethinking the connections between campus courses and field experiences in college- and university-based teacher education. *Journal of Teacher Education*, 61(1–2), 89–99.

Index

For Product Safety Concerns and Information please contact our EU
representative GPSR@taylorandfrancis.com
Taylor & Francis Verlag GmbH, Kaufingerstraße 24, 80331 München, Germany

www.ingramcontent.com/pod-product-compliance
Lightning Source LLC
Chambersburg PA
CBHW050520280326
41932CB00014B/2399

9 781138 289772